Valuation of Indian Life Insurance Companies

Valuation of Indian Life Insurance Companies

Prasanna Rajesh

BEP BUSINESS EXPERT PRESS

First published in 2019 by
Business Expert Press, LLC
222 East 46th Street, New York, NY 10017
www.businessexpertpress.com

ISBN-13: 978-1-94999-152-9 (paperback)
ISBN-13: 978-1-94999-153-6 (e-book)

Business Expert Press Finance and Financial Management Collection

Collection ISSN: 2331-0049 (print)
Collection ISSN: 2331-0057 (electronic)

Cover and interior design by S4Carlisle Publishing Services Private Ltd., Chennai, India

First edition: 2019

10 9 8 7 6 5 4 3 2 1

Printed in the United States of America.

Abstract

This book bridges the gap between the accounting and the actuarial sides of Indian life insurance companies. It explores the relationships between the embedded value calculated by actuaries and the revenue account and balance sheet prepared by the accountants. It uses publicly available sources of information to place a value on the shares of Indian life insurance companies from an outsider's point of view.

Life insurance company accounts are complex and need understanding of a few concepts in order to analyze and appreciate them. This book helps a lay person with reasonable numerical abilities to gauge and understand the reasoning behind the calculation of the share price of a life insurance company. In particular, it will help analysts and accountants with no actuarial background to understand the concepts of embedded and appraisal value.

Cash flow statements of these companies are often ignored and delegated to the background or usually to a single page in their annual reports. This book looks at the cash flows in detail and rearranges them to get a better picture of the financial health of the underlying companies. It also explains the relationship between the different measures of profit such as cash reserves, surplus, profit after tax, and embedded value.

Very often, a lot of this information is only available internally within the life insurance companies or to their consultants. This book uses alternative approaches based purely on public disclosures by these companies thereby enables professionals without access to internal information to come to informed judgments about the actual performance of the companies.

Keywords

Indian insurance companies; accounting; finance; embedded value; appraisal value; cash flow; surplus; profits

Contents

Acknowledgments

National Library Board, Singapore for access to wonderful books, Timothy Jury, for his insightful book on cash flows and my family, for their love and patience.

CHAPTER 1

Indian Insurance Companies

Introduction

1.1. This chapter explains how insurance companies differ from other companies and also looks at the challenges faced by them. It gives a brief history of the private players and touches on the diversity of the Indian insurance market. It also lists the kinds of published financial information available and specifies the basic structure of this information.

How are insurance companies different from other companies?

1.2. Insurance companies, just like other companies, sell their products to the general public and expect to profit from them. Therein ends the similarity, however, because insurance products are by nature very different from the products sold by companies in other industries.

1.3. Insurance companies collect premiums for a long time before the benefits become due, which means that profits or losses can be known only after the policies go off the books.

1.4. Also, profits or losses can be assessed only for groups of policies and not individual ones, because the meaning of insurance is that groups of people come together and subsidize one another in the event of a claim. This makes the calculations very complicated but interesting.

1.5. This also means that general rules and regulations are inadequate and we need special rules to monitor these companies.

How easy and how profitable is it to sell insurance?

1.6. This is the basic question that a prospective shareholder must ask. The answer to this question will determine whether she is willing to invest in the business. The common perception is that insurance is easy money. Nothing can be farther from the truth. This industry is one of the most difficult to do business in and also one of the most profitable. Here is a phrase commonly used in this industry: "Insurance is sold, not bought." Most *financially savvy* people only know that they hold a life insurance policy with a particular company and are completely unaware of the details of the policy they have bought.

1.7. To sell an insurance product to persons who are financially unaware, the companies have to first make them aware that they need insurance, and then convince them to part with their money for a number of years, in return for a benefit payment many years later.

1.8. Many have a change of heart as soon as the product is sold. This is the reason why there is a free look period (usually about 15 days) during which customers can take their money back without any questions asked and also the reason why there are high lapse rates in the very first policy year. Sometimes, this rate is as high as 30 percent. Companies lose the most in this first year of operation if the policy lapses, mainly because they experience very high costs in this first year, usually more than the premium collected. Once the companies are past the first-year hurdle, the challenge is to make sure that the policyholder keeps the policy in force and continues to pay the premium year on year.

1.9. If we assume the average term of a policy to be 20 years, the company has to keep the policyholder committed for 20 years. During this time, if the policyholder decides to surrender the policy, the company has to pay the surrender value, which may or may not cover the expenses, and make a profit. The company may not have to pay a surrender value if the policy is surrendered within, say, the first three years, but even without a surrender payment, it makes a loss if the expenses are not fully recovered. Surrenders also depend on the movements in the stock market and general financial conditions. In addition, there will be competition from other players in the market. Combine this with the basic distrust of anything private, and these companies have their work cut out. Factoring all this in, the business is not an easy one.

1.10. Assuming that the company overcomes all the aforementioned problems, the business is a very profitable one and rewards the shareholders more than adequately for the risks taken. Just how profitable the business is, varies from market to market and from company to company.

What is the history of private insurance companies in the Indian insurance market?

1.11. The history of Indian Insurance is set out in detail in the website of Insurance Regulatory And Development Authority of India (IRDA). The Indian insurance industry was opened to private players in the year 2000, after a very long time. Until then, the Life Insurance Corporation of India, with the brand name LIC, was synonymous with life insurance and the General Insurance Corporation of India, GIC in short, was synonymous with general insurance. There were no stand-alone health insurance companies at all in the market.

1.12. Now there are as many as 24 life insurance companies and 34 nonlife and health insurance companies. Some of these companies entered the market in the year 2000 and have in the recent past had initial public offerings (IPOs) of their shares.

What is the size of the Indian insurance market?

1.13. The annual reports and accounts of all the companies talk about how underinsured India is and claim that the growth in the industry, and by default, their company's growth is expected to be sky high. This needs to be taken with a pinch of salt because even if the ocean is vast, their collection can be only as big as their pail. Another point is, do they want the ocean?

1.14. Just for the sake of argument, if we assume that the whole of India is available to be insured and the companies only have to nod their heads to get the business, would they rush into it? Without any doubt, they would want to cherry-pick the profitable portions of the business. What then is this profitable percentage of the entire population? My calculated guess is that it is not a very high percentage because not all of India has witnessed economic growth in the same measure. Some parts of India are economically forward and financially savvy than most others, more likely the cities, and the competition in these areas with the other insurance companies is usually cutthroat. This competition may bring down the profitability of the business written. Socio cultural norms also may play a very important role in the purchase of insurance contracts. For example, the joint family system is no longer as prevalent in cities as it was in the past. This has increased the need for insurance in nuclear families and has opened up the market some more. It is too early to comment whether the insurance industry has already capitalized on these new social norms. The insurance companies also need infrastructure to penetrate untapped markets, which will eat up a lot of capital and also may not be as profitable. To sum it all up, the size of the insurance market is a small percentage of India, rather than the entire country as it is made out to be.

What kind of growth can we expect in insurance? Is the industry similar to the information technology (IT) industry, where some companies had phenomenal growth, or is it more similar to the auto industry, where you need to set up considerable infrastructure to get a modest level of growth?

1.15. This sector is unique and very different from the IT sector, where the biggest investment is in human capital. This is also different from the auto sector, where you need to set up huge factories. The closest sector that is comparable to insurance is banking, but then again, because of the nature of products sold, even this sector is markedly different. As I mentioned earlier, the insurance sector was opened to private players in 2000, after a very long time. The companies that I will be analyzing in the following chapters are the earliest ones that started doing business in India. We therefore do not have any other companies that can be used as historical reference points. These are also the very first to come out with IPO's. LIC falls in a very different category and cannot be used for comparison.

1.16. All this put together means that insurance is quite unlike any other industry and India is quite unlike any other market and so it is also not as easy to succeed here as it is perceived or made out to be.

How do we assess the profitability of these private insurance companies?

1.17. Here is where the published information comes in handy. Our starting point for this would be to collect relevant information that is easily available and then choose those bits that will help us in our analysis of the profitability of the companies.

What is the published information available?

1.18. The IRDA monitors insurance companies in India. It also specifies all the guidelines and reports that need to be published and amends these rules and regulations to reflect changing scenarios.

1.19. The published information is very much like those of all other companies and consists of the following:
   a. Revenue Account or Policyholders' Technical Account
   b. Profit and Loss Account or Shareholders' Non-technical Account
   c. Balance Sheet
   d. Receipts and Payments Account
   e. Schedules accompanying the financial statements
   f. Embedded Value Report
   g. Red herring prospectus
   h. Parent company's website

1.19.1. The first five are published every year in the company's annual report. Some of the information is also available quarterly on the company's website.

1.19.2. Not all companies publish their Embedded Value Report and if available, it is only for the years after the IPO.

1.19.3. The red herring prospectus is available on the Securities and Exchange Board of India (SEBI) website and is published just before the IPO. The red herring prospectus is beyond the scope of this book, and I will be using only tiny bits of it. It is an exhaustive document and runs into many pages. Anyone interested in understanding insurance risks and the Indian market in detail must take a look at this document.

1.19.4. Parent companies sometimes reveal information about their subsidiaries to their investors on a quarterly basis. This again is another valuable source of information.

How is the accounting structure different for Indian insurance companies?

1.20. To explain the accounting structure, we have to first understand the concept of funds. There are essentially two funds in a life insurance company in India. By two funds I mean that the business can be split into two groups because the share of profits to the shareholders is different for each group. Once the profits or surplus for each group are calculated, they are added to determine the overall surplus of the company. The two funds can be described as follows:

a. Par fund (short for participating fund)

The profits arising in this fund are split between the policyholders and the shareholders in a predetermined percentage, 90/10, where the policyholders' share is 90% and the shareholders' share is 10%. The IRDA defines the shareholders' share of surplus as one-ninth of the surplus allocated to policyholders.

b. Non-par fund (short for non-participating fund)

Here the shareholders get all the surplus, hence this is also called the 0/100 fund.

1.21. These two funds are further split into the following:
   a. Linked business, including variable insurance products for life, general annuity, pensions, and health insurance
   b. Non-linked business, including variable insurance products for life, general annuity, pensions, and health insurance
   c. Health insurance, separately for retail, group, and government scheme
   d. Business within India and business outside India

Companies do not write all the lines of businesses mentioned in the subgroups, so the total number of subgroups in the Revenue Account is usually between 5 and 10. Generally, linked and health businesses are written only in the non-par fund. So, depending on the products sold by the company, the Revenue Account and Balance Sheet are split to show the different funds and subfunds the products are written in.

1.22. Now that the basic accounting structure is defined, we move on to the format of information available.
   1.22.1. *Revenue Account or the Policyholders' Technical Account*
      1.22.1.1. The Revenue Account or Policyholders' Technical Account is usually in the form of

         Premium
         less Reinsurance premium
         plus Income from investments
         less Commission
         less Expenses other than commission (includes provision for income tax and service tax)
         less Benefits
         less Increase in reserves (I will explain this in Chapter 3)
         = Surplus arising in the year

      1.22.1.2. This surplus will be divided between the shareholders and policyholders depending on the fund in which the products are written. The company also needs to hold extensive information on the expenses incurred because all expenses have to be split between the different funds of the company. Commission is usually product specific, and this can be linked straightaway to the product and consequently to the fund. Others are not so clear, for example, advertising. All the products benefit from advertising, so the expenses need to be apportioned to the different lines of businesses. This is an exercise by itself and it is the responsibility of the company to segment the transactions into the different funds in a fair manner so that no one group benefits at the expense of another. These segmental Revenue Accounts are added to form the consolidated Revenue Account or the Policyholders' Technical Account.

1.22.1.3. The shareholders' share of the surplus from this Revenue Account will be fed into the Shareholders' Non-technical Account and the total profit or loss for the shareholders will be determined in this account.

1.22.2. *Profit and Loss Account or the Shareholders' Non-technical Account*

1.22.2.1. The Shareholders' Non-technical Account will usually be as follows:

Surplus transferred from the Revenue Account

plus Income from investments in the shareholders' fund

less Expenses in the shareholders' fund

equals Profit Before Tax (PBT)

less provision for tax

equals Profit After Tax (PAT)

This is the profit or loss the company has estimated for the year.

1.22.3. *Balance Sheet*

    1.22.3.1. The liabilities will have the following:

        Shareholders' reserves

        Policyholders' reserves

        Funds for future appropriations

        The assets will have the following:

        Shareholders' investments

        Policyholders' investments

        Loans

        Fixed assets

        Net current assets

1.22.4. *Receipts and Payments Account*

    1.22.4.1. This is the Cash Flow statement of the company and companies have to use the direct method. This consists of three sections: cash flow from operating activities, cash flow from investing activities, and cash flow from financing activities. I have explained this format in detail in Chapter 5.

1.22.5. *Schedules*

    1.22.5.1. There will also be schedules accompanying these statements, where each of the account heads in the Revenue Account and Balance Sheet will be dealt with in more detail.

1.22.6. *Embedded Value Report*

    1.22.6.1. This report splits the embedded value (I will cover this later in Chapter 8) into its components and also talks about how it has changed from one year to the next. It sets out the assumptions used for the calculation and explores the sensitivity of the embedded value to a change in the assumptions.

1.22.7. *Red Herring Prospectus*

    1.22.7.1. The red herring prospectus is available on the SEBI website. It is an extensive document and provides details of the IPO. The Embedded

Value Report also forms a part of the prospectus. Most importantly, this document enumerates all the risks associated with the business and provides a very comprehensive idea of the factors affecting the profitability of the business. It is published only once and just before the IPO.

Conclusion

1.23. Now that we have a fair idea of the published framework, we will move on to the next chapter, which uses this information. We start off by looking at the amount of money invested to start these companies and compare this with the share price.

CHAPTER 2

Capital Injections and Market Capitalization

Introduction

2.1. In this chapter and all the following chapters, we will analyze the published accounts of three companies: HDFC Life (HDFC Life), ICICI Prudential Life (ICICI Pru), and SBI Life (SBI Life). ICICI Pru was the first company in the life insurance private sector to have an IPO, in 2016, followed by HDFC Life in 2017 and then SBI Life in 2017.

2.2. We start by looking at the capital injected in each of these three companies from inception to the date of the IPO and then compare the accumulated value of this capital with the IPO price to get the internal rate of return (IRR). We, therefore, deal only with what has happened in the past and look at only one aspect of the business—the capital injected into the company. We will also calculate the share price assuming the capital had accumulated at a rate different from the IRR to get a different picture to the one presented by the IPO.

2.3. You may ask now, who looks at how much money has been put in to start a business, and more importantly, you may want to know the answer to the question in the following section.

Is the capital injected into the company relevant today?

2.4. Generally, the capital put into the company is rarely considered when analysts place a value on the share. Indian private insurance companies, however, started operations only in 2000, when the insurance sector was privatized, so because we are talking of a time span of less than 20 years (2000 to 2017), the capital invested to start the companies is very much relevant today. This amount can then be the figure we first start with and we can use this as an indicator of the value of the company.

How do we get the net capital movement in each year?

2.5. The total capital in the company at the end of any financial year is the sum of the share capital account and the share premium account. The capital injected over the year is then the difference between the end year and beginning year figures of the sum of the share premium and share capital accounts. Subtracting the dividend paid over the year from this gives us the net capital movement during the year. The dividend here is the proposed dividend, including any interim dividend in the profit and loss account, and not the actual dividend paid. Since the annual reports and accounts are unavailable for the earliest years, I have assumed that the capital injected in those years was done on the first day of operation.

Now that we have this figure for each year of operation, what do we do with it?

2.6. We look at the company as a single entity and try and equate the capital movements to the market capitalization of the company. The connecting factor is the IRR, and this is the rate of return assumed to be earned year on year on the capital, so that the total equals the market capitalization.

How is the IRR calculated?

2.7. Multiplying the IPO share price with the number of shares in the Balance Sheet as on that date will give us a figure for the total market capitalization of the company. The accumulated capital value is then equated to this market capitalization of the company at a rate of interest allowing for the dates of capital movement.

The rate of interest that equates the accumulated value of the capital injected in each year to the market capitalization on the eve of the IPO is the IRR. This is a simple calculation using an excel spreadsheet. We now calculate the IRR for all the three companies (Tables 2.1, 2.2, and 2.3).

Table 2.1 IRR for HDFC LIFE

	Total number of shares	1,998,475,283	IRR	31.66%
	Market cap at 275 per share	549,580,702,825		
Year	**Share capital at year end**	**Share premium at year end**	**Dividend paid over the year**	**Net capital movement in the year**
2000	3,200,000,000			3,200,000,000
2005	3,200,000,000			0
2006	6,200,000,000			3,000,000,000
2007	8,012,609,100			1,812,609,100
2008	12,710,000,000			4,697,390,900
2009	17,960,000,000			5,250,000,000
2010	19,680,000,000			1,720,000,000
2011	19,948,800,960	1,654,372,000		1,923,172,960
2012	19,948,800,960	1,654,372,000		0
2013	19,948,800,960	1,654,372,000		0
2014	19,948,800,960	1,654,372,000	997,440,000	-997,440,000
2015	19,948,800,960	1,654,372,000	1,396,416,000	-1,396,416,000
2016	19,952,881,380	1,687,015,000	1,795,403,000	-1,758,679,580
2017	19,984,752,830	1,944,058,000	2,197,413,000	-1,908,498,550
			market cap on IPO date	549,580,702,825

Numbers and amounts at actuals

Table 2.2 IRR for ICICI Pru

	Total number of shares	1,432,319,348	IRR	22.46%
	Market cap at 300 per share	429,695,804,400		
Year	Share capital at year end	Share premium at year end	Dividend paid over the year	Net capital movement in the year
2000	11,850,000,000			11,850,000,000
2006	11,850,000,000			0
2007	13,123,015,350	7,593,813,000		8,866,828,350
2008	14,011,137,230	23,713,076,000		17,007,384,880
2009	14,272,572,930	33,529,185,000		10,077,544,700
2010	14,281,428,830	33,588,365,000		68,035,900
2011	14,284,611,490	33,606,925,000		21,742,660
2012	14,288,491,240	33,639,515,000	4,143,662,000	-4,107,192,250
2013	14,289,392,490	33,645,103,000	4,843,294,000	-4,836,804,750
2014	14,292,556,870	33,663,847,000	10,932,954,000	-10,911,045,620
2015	14,317,169,910	33,838,435,000	8,368,252,000	-8,169,050,960
2016	14,323,193,480	33,897,405,000	12,029,941,000	-11,964,947,430
			market cap on IPO date	429,695,804,400

Numbers and amounts at actuals

Table 2.3 IRR for SBI Life

	Total number of shares	1,000,000,000	IRR	36.44%
	Market cap at 700 per share	700,000,000,000		
Year	Share capital at year end	Share premium at year end	Dividend paid over the year	Net capital movement in the year
2001	4,250,000,000			4,250,000,000
2005	4,250,000,000			0
2006	4,250,000,000			0
2007	5,000,000,000			750,000,000
2008	10,000,000,000			5,000,000,000
2009	10,000,000,000			0
2010	10,000,000,000			0

Table 2.3 IRR for SBI Life (Continued)

Year	Share capital at year end	Share premium at year end	Dividend paid over the year	Net capital movement in the year
2011	10,000,000,000			0
2012	10,000,000,000		500,000,000	-500,000,000
2013	10,000,000,000		500,000,000	-500,000,000
2014	10,000,000,000		1,000,000,000	-1,000,000,000
2015	10,000,000,000		1,200,000,000	-1,200,000,000
2016	10,000,000,000		1,200,000,000	-1,200,000,000
2017	10,000,000,000		1,500,000,000	-1,500,000,000
			Market cap on IPO date	700,000,000,000

Numbers and amounts at actuals

What do the IRR figures mean?

2.8.   HDFC Life has an IRR of 31.6 percent for a share price of Rs 275, ICICI Pru has a 22.4 percent IRR for a share price of Rs 300, and SBI Life has a 36.4 percent IRR for a share price of Rs 700.

2.9.   Let us analyze the results in more detail. Are these IRRs justified? What have these companies done with the capital to achieve the value indicated by the IRR? To answer this question, we first need a benchmark rate of return.

2.10. The rate of return expected on a particular share is the sum of the following:

a.   The risk free rate or the rate of return if you invest in gilts for, say, 10 years.

b.   The risk associated with the industry. In our case, it is the insurance industry in India.

c.   The risk associated with this particular company.

2.11. The risk free rate can be assumed to be around 8 percent. This rate, plus a rate of another 7 percent for points (b) and (c), gives 15 percent. (I have assumed the same risk for all three companies; in practice, the market will use different rates.) In other words, my estimate for the return on capital for any of the companies above would be about 15 percent, or if I am being very optimistic, I would use a 20 percent rate of return.

2.12. I would then start from this rate of return and assess the results using this benchmark. Using 20 percent as the benchmark rate of return on capital, all the three companies seem to be overpriced, with SBI Life taking the lead, closely followed by HDFC Life. ICICI Pru seems more reasonably priced with the IRR at 22.4 percent.

2.13. This view, however, has one major drawback: We are only looking at the past and have not factored in the future at all. Should not the share price also reflect what profits the company is expected to make in the future? The profits expected depend on the industry first and the company second. Before we look at the future, however, let us have a relook at the past and try to guess what the share price would be if the IRR had been in line with industry norms and if we leave future expectations out of the equation. This leads us to the next question.

What will the share price be for a different IRR?

2.14. We can also perform the above exercise the other way round. We find the total value of the company and consequently the share price for a defined IRR. This is done by first accumulating the capital injected up to the IPO date at one particular rate of interest. This accumulated value is then divided by the number of shares as on that date to give the share price. The results are as given in Table 2.4.

Table 2.4. Calculated share prices for different IRRs

IRR	HDFC Life	ICICI Pru	SBI Life
15%	45.05	119.24	52.53
20%	77.80	223.40	100.34

2.15. We now find that these rates are way below the IPO price and the share price quoted in the market. How are these rates so different from the market price? At this point, you may be tempted to ask, surely an insurance company is very different from a used car? Do we find out what has been paid for an asset and then derive a value from there or do we forget the past and see what the company is expected to do in the future? Or we may rephrase this question to what is the investor paying for— the growth in the past, the expected growth in the future, or the brand name?

Composition of the share price

2.16. The share price is a combination of what has happened in the past and what is expected in the future. This means that the share price is roughly made up of three components:
   a. Past growth
   b. Future growth
   c. Goodwill

2.17. The investor has to apportion the share price into these three parts and then take a call on whether she is in agreement with what the market has priced the share. This is required so that the investor has no doubt in her mind about the value of the product she is buying, the risks associated with it, and consequently, the impact on the share price if the future is not as expected.

How do we apportion the share price into these three components?

2.18. The value calculated earlier may be assumed to be that portion of the share price which reflects the growth of the company up to the date of the IPO. There are more accurate methods of doing this calculation, however, instead of the previous ad hoc calculation. This leads us to the concepts of embedded value and appraisal value, which are unique to insurance and which will give us an idea of the different components of the share price.

CHAPTER 3

Embedded Value and Appraisal Value

Introduction

3.1. In this chapter, I will define two terms—embedded value and appraisal value— discuss how they are calculated, and specify their relation to the share price of the company.

What is embedded value?

3.2. Simply put, embedded value is the total value to the shareholders of the business currently on the company's books. This value is the sum of all the profits the shareholders will earn in the future from the in-force policies discounted to the present date and the value of the extra assets that belong to the shareholders. This calculation makes no allowance for the future business that the company will write and looks at only the policies in the company's books.

What are the basic differences between the share price of an ordinary company and the embedded value of an insurance company?

3.3. Let us consider a company in the manufacturing industry. The share price of this company is based on the profits the company will earn from the goods that the company will sell in the future. A part of the share price will be the brand value of the company. There are no profits from the goods sold in the past.

3.4. In insurance companies, profits arise in the future from policies sold in the past. The value of these profits, plus the extra assets in the fund, is the embedded value. In these calculations, the policies that will be sold in the future and the profits arising from those policies are not considered at all.

How is embedded value calculated?

3.5. Embedded value is found by projecting the cash flows of all the policies currently in the company's books into the future and discounting the shareholders' share of the profits to the present date. To this value of in-force policies, the extra assets in the fund that belong to the shareholders are added, to arrive at the embedded value.

3.6. A lot of assumptions go into this calculation. In simple terms, we have to project each and every item in the Revenue Account and Shareholders' Non-technical Account into the future, find the profits in each year, and then discount the profits back to the present date. For this exercise, we have to split the profits arising in the future into two groups, the first being the profits from the policies that are on the books already and the second the profits on the new business that the company will write in each future year. For the time being, we will ignore the future new business because the embedded value is the value of the profits of the existing business only.

3.7. We will, therefore, have to estimate, among other things, how many policies will be in force, what is the mortality expected, when and what other decrements (like lapses/surrenders) are expected, what is the interest that the company will earn, and what are the reserves the company will have to hold for these policies. Reserves are the sums companies hold to meet future liabilities. The expenses assumption also forms an important aspect of this projection, and we will assume that the company is open to new business, although the profits from the new business will not be accounted for in this calculation.

3.8. There are basically two methods.

Method 1

3.8.1. One of the methods of calculating embedded value is to use a policy-by-policy approach. This means that we chalk out the cash flows of each and every policy, allowing for mortality, expenses, expected interest to be earned, valuation reserves, surrenders, lapses, taxation, and so on, and then discount the profit of each policy back to the present date. An investor will be unable to do this for many reasons, chief among them being the following:

a. She does not have the data.
b. The calculations are very complicated.
c. She does not know the surrender experience, mortality experience, and so on.
d. Valuation reserves also have to be calculated.
e. Volumes are huge.

Method 2

3.8.2. A second method is to use model points. This method first groups the policies into homogenous groups. Each group is represented by sample points, and these sample points are used to roughly estimate the embedded value. This will reduce the volume of the calculations as only representative policies will be used in the calculations. This is again a fairly complicated process and has many of the problems outlined above.

3.9. This only shows that the embedded value calculation is beyond the capabilities of an ordinary investor and that she has to rely on the embedded value quoted in the company's accounts.

What are the components of the embedded value?

3.10. The embedded value is expressed as the sum of value of in force (VIF) and the adjusted net worth (ANW). In India, it is called as the Indian embedded value or IEV.

$$IEV = VIF + ANW$$

3.10.1. VIF is the present value at the valuation date of future profits expected from all the in-force business. The company will first project the future profits and then discount them to the valuation date.

3.10.2. ANW is the balance assets left in the funds that belong to the shareholders.

Where is the embedded value available?

3.11. The embedded value is available in the annual report and accounts along with the VIF and ANW. The change in the embedded value from one year to the next is analyzed and split into various components and presented along with the breakup of the embedded value into ANW and VIF at the beginning and the end of the year.

3.12. Some companies also publish the Embedded Value report, although this is not mandatory. Companies have to vet this embedded value calculation with an independent actuary but this report is not published. A copy of this report is available in the red herring prospectus. This information, again, is available only for the years after the IPO and not before.

How is the embedded value used?

3.13. The companies simply quote the embedded value, analyze how it has grown over the year, split the growth into its various components, talk about the growth rate, and then leave it at that.

3.14. Although companies quote the total embedded value, they almost never quote the embedded value per share. If they do so, the difference between the share price and the embedded value per share will be immediately obvious and it will also prompt an analyst to ask the next question as to why there is such a huge difference between the two figures. Having said this, you may be wondering if there is some relationship between the embedded value and the share price.

Is there a relationship between the embedded value and share price?

3.15. Because the embedded value is the shareholders' share of future profits, there is a relationship between the embedded value and the share price. What then is missing in the above equation?

3.16. It is the value of the profits of future new business the company will write. If this is added to the embedded value, this will give the total profits expected from the current as well as future policies. This is called the appraisal value of the company.

$$\text{Appraisal value} = \text{Embedded value} + \text{Value of future new business}$$

3.17. We can then arrive at an estimate of the share price by dividing the appraisal value by the number of shares at the valuation date.

$$\text{Share price} = \text{Appraisal value}/\text{number of shares}$$

How is appraisal value calculated and where is it available?

3.18. Just by itself, the embedded value calculation is a very complicated one. To this complication, if you add the future new business, with additional sets of assumptions for the future, the results may be very subjective and the effort may not justify the results or the reliability of the calculation.

3.19. Companies also would have a lot of leeway in quoting a very high appraisal value by a very small tweak in the future assumptions. This would become an administrative nightmare for the regulator.

3.20. So, companies do not quote this value in their accounts although they may do these projections internally. The independent actuary's report also states that it comments only on the embedded value and does not talk about the appraisal value.

3.21. The appraisal value is usually calculated by a rule of thumb used worldwide. It is expressed as a multiple of the embedded value.

In Asia, this multiple is generally 2. *Higher the multiple, higher is the reliance on the future business, and consequently, more optimistic is the share price.*

3.22. One method of calculating the share price is to calculate the embedded value per share and then multiply this by 2. Using this method, the share prices for the three companies are

HDFC Life

Embedded value per share = Embedded value/number of shares in the company.
HDFC LIFE embedded value per share on March 31, 2018

$$= 15216 / 2{,}011{,}740{,}043 \times 10{,}000{,}000$$
$$= 75.64 \text{ per share}$$
$$\text{Estimated share price} = 2 \times 75.64 = 151.28$$

(I have multiplied by 10,000,000 because the embedded value is in crores.)
(For ICICI Pru and SBI Life, I have multiplied by 1 billion because the embedded value is in billions.)

ICICI Pru

ICICI PRU embedded value per share on March 31, 2018

$$= 187.88 / 1{,}435{,}498{,}710 \times 1{,}000{,}000{,}000$$
$$= 130.88 \text{ per share}$$
$$\text{Estimated share price} = 2 \times 130.88 = 261.76$$

SBI Life

SBI Life embedded value per share on March 31, 2018

$$= 190.7 / 1{,}000{,}000{,}000 \times 1{,}000{,}000{,}000$$
$$= 190.7 \text{ per share}$$
$$\text{Estimated share price} = 2 \times 190.7 = 381.4$$

3.23. It is interesting to see how these figures compare with those in the previous chapter. HDFC Life IPO share price is Rs 275, whereas our calculated appraisal value is Rs 151.28. ICICI Pru's IPO price is Rs 300 and our calculated appraisal value is Rs 261.76. SBI Life's IPO share price is Rs 700 and our calculated appraisal value is Rs 381.74. The calculated appraisal value of only ICICI Pru seems reasonably close to the IPO share price.

3.24. The share prices calculated here have inched upward from those calculated in Table 2.4 in the previous chapter but are again very different from the quoted share prices.

3.25. The difference between the appraisal value per share and the share price is then the brand value or goodwill of the company.

What is the current multiple used in the share price?

3.26. The appraisal value multiple implicit in the share price also depends on the buoyancy of the stock market. If the market is in a euphoric state, as it is currently (January 2019), investors usually are in an upbeat mood and will be willing to pay a price that is way above the norm. In the Table 3.1, I have calculated the appraisal value multiple as on December 31, 2018.

Table 3.1 Appraisal value multiple

	Embedded value per share on March 31, 2018	Closing share price on December 31, 2018	Appraisal value multiple
HDFC Life	75.64	387.55	5.12
ICICI Pru	130.88	323.90	2.47
SBI Life	190.70	596.45	3.13

Share prices are from Bombay Stock Exchange (BSE).

What do the numbers in Table 3.1 mean?

3.27. The appraisal value multiple for HDFC Life is 5.12, which is way above the norm. This means that the brand HDFC Life holds a lot of value and the general public is willing to pay this high price for the brand. The other two are also above the mean value of 2, but the share prices are more reasonable compared with that of HDFC Life.

3.28. There is a timing mismatch between the embedded value per share date and the share price date. Embedded value is available only on financial year end dates in the annual report of the companies. On December 31, 2018, the embedded value will most likely (unless the company operates at a loss) be higher than the one used. This means that the embedded value multiple will be lesser than what is calculated. My guess is that it will not be drastically different from the ones calculated. This table aims to only give us a feel for the multiple, rather than place an exact value.

Conclusion

3.29. The important point to remember is that the investor is paying for business that is currently not in the company's books, that is, she is paying for the future new business of the company. If the appraisal value is four times the embedded value, 75 percent of the share price reflects future new business and brand value and only 25 percent is for the profits expected from existing business. How each investor views this piece of information depends on how she believes the future will pan out.

3.30. Our next question is, what is the growth rate expected to be achieved in the future for the share price to be justified? In other words, we need some numbers to talk about instead of just future growth. If we assign some numbers to this growth rate, we may be able to judge for ourselves whether this is achievable. For this, we now move on to the next chapter, which puts a value to this growth rate.

CHAPTER 4

Growth Rate in the Share Price Using VNB, NBM, APE

Introduction

4.1. This chapter first defines some of the profit indicators the Indian insurance companies use in their annual reports and then demonstrates how to use them to measure the growth rate inherent in the current share price.

What are the profit indicators used by Indian insurance companies?

4.2. Companies often flaunt the following in their annual reports and to use them we first need to understand them.

New Business Margin (NBM)

4.2.1. NBM is a percentage measure of profitability computed as the present value of future profits on the business sourced in a particular period, usually a year, and denoted as a percentage of annualized premium equivalent.

Annualized Premium Equivalent (APE)

4.2.2. This is the sum of annualized first-year regular premiums and 10 percent of single premiums and 10 percent of single premium top-ups. It gives us a rough idea of the annualized new business premium for the year.

Value of New Business (VNB)

    4.2.3. This value is quoted in almost all annual reports and is the shareholders' share of the profits of the new business written in the year.

This can also be expressed as

$$NBM * APE.$$

For example, if the NBM is 20 percent, the VNB = 20 percent * APE

    4.2.4. If we know the VNB and the NBM, we can work backward and then calculate the APE for this particular year. Therefore,

$$APE = VNB/NBM$$

Calculating the share price using APE, VNB, NBM, and embedded value

4.3. In the previous chapter, I explained that

Share price = Appraisal value/number of shares

where

Appraisal value = Embedded value
+ Value of profits from future new business

therefore,

Share price = (Embedded value + Value of profits from future new business)/number of shares

Or, the same equation can be re-expressed as

Value of profits from future new business = Share price × number of shares − Embedded value

From these equations we can either calculate the share price for a particular growth rate or keep the share price fixed and find the growth rate that hits this share price.

4.4. Let us first fix the growth rate and then find the share price for this growth rate. For this, we have to first find the profits from the future new business. This is done by projecting the new business premium in each future year, finding the profits from that premium on that date, and then discounting those profits to the present date. This is where we use the APE, NBM, and VNB, and the process is described next.

    a. The first step in the five-step process is the projection of the new business premium in each future year. For that, we need a base on which we will build the future premiums using a growth factor. This base is the current year's APE. This is calculated by dividing the VNB by the NBM for the current year.

    b. Once we have the APE for the current year, we incorporate a growth factor, say 20 percent, into this APE and find the APE for each future year. I have assumed a 20-year time horizon, but this also is a variable and can be changed.

    c. The APE for each future year calculated in step (b) should then be multiplied with the NBM to get the profits from that tranche of new business. This gives us a value of the profits the company expects to make from that tranche on that particular date. In this case, we assume that the NBM does not change and remains constant from one year to the next.

    d. These profits are, however, the profits on that date. They have to be discounted to the present date using a discount factor. The discount factor is defined as $(1/(1 + i))\,\wedge\, n$, where i is the discount rate and n is the number of years to the present date. This discount factor, like the growth factor and the total number of years, can be kept variable and we can change it to find the impact on the share price. As a starting point, I have assumed this discount rate to be 15 percent.

e. The final step is to keep changing the growth rate and finding the share price to assess the sensitivity of the share price to changing scenarios.

4.5. This process is best explained with an example.

HDFC Life

NBM = 23.2 percent

VNB = 1,282 (in crores) or 12,820 (in millions)

(These figures are from HDFC Life's annual report of 2017 through 2018.)

Therefore, calculated APE = 12,820/23.2 * 100

= 55,258.6 (in millions)

4.5.1. This is the APE for 2018 from which the company expects to make a profit of 12,820. Table 4.1 shows the calculation of the share price by estimating future new business and calculating the profits arising from this future new business. This is done by assuming that the APE grows by 20 percent year on year, NBM remains constant at 23.2 percent for all the years, and the profits are discounted back to the present date at 15 percent.

Table 4.1 Calculation of HDFC Life share price March 31, 2018

Year	APE Base year	Percentage inc in premium 20%	Profit = NBM @ 23.2%* APE	Disc factor @ 15%	Present value of profit in each year
1	55259	66,310	15,384	0.8696	13,377
2		79,572	18,461	0.7561	13,959
3		95,487	22,153	0.6575	14,566
4		114,584	26,584	0.5718	15,199
5		137,501	31,900	0.4972	15,860
6		165,001	38,280	0.4323	16,550

Year	APE Base year	Percentage inc in premium 20%	Profit = NBM @ 23.2%* APE	Disc factor @ 15%	Present value of profit in each year
7		198,002	45,936	0.3759	17,269
8		237,602	55,124	0.3269	18,020
9		285,122	66,148	0.2843	18,803
10		342,147	79,378	0.2472	19,621
11		410,576	95,254	0.2149	20,474
12		492,691	114,304	0.1869	21,364
13		591,230	137,165	0.1625	22,293
14		709,476	164,598	0.1413	23,262
15		851,371	197,518	0.1229	24,274
16		1,021,645	237,022	0.1069	25,329
17		1,225,974	284,426	0.0929	26,431
18		1,471,169	341,311	0.0808	27,580
19		1,765,402	409,573	0.0703	28,779
20		2,118,483	491,488	0.0611	30,030
			Total PV of	future profits	413,041
				EV	152,160
				AV	565,201
				share price	280.95

Amounts in millions except share price in actuals
PV is the present value
EV is the embedded value on March 31, 2018 (HDFC Life annual report 2017-2018)
AV is the calculated appraisal value on March 31, 2018

4.5.2. The share price works out to Rs 280.95.

4.5.3. If we change the growth in APE to 25 percent, keeping other assumptions the same, the share price works out to Rs 418.13. So, to justify a share price of Rs 418.13, the company has to increase its APE by 25 percent year on year.

ICICI Pru

NBM = 16.5 percent

VNB = 12.86 (in billions) or 12,860 (in millions)

APE = 77.92 billion or 77,920 million.

NBM, VNB and APE figures are from ICICI Pru annual report 2017-2018 (Table 4.2).

Table 4.2 Calculation of ICICI Pru share price on March 31, 2018

Year	APE Base year	Percentage inc in premium 20%	Profit = NBM @16.5% * APE	Disc factor @ 15%	Present value of profit in each year
1	77920	93,504	15,428	0.8696	13,416
2		112,205	18,514	0.7561	13,999
3		134,646	22,217	0.6575	14,608
4		161,575	26,660	0.5718	15,243
5		193,890	31,992	0.4972	15,906
6		232,668	38,390	0.4323	16,597
7		279,201	46,068	0.3759	17,319
8		335,042	55,282	0.3269	18,072
9		402,050	66,338	0.2843	18,857
10		482,460	79,606	0.2472	19,677
11		578,952	95,527	0.2149	20,533
12		694,743	114,633	0.1869	21,426
13		833,691	137,559	0.1625	22,357
14		1,000,429	165,071	0.1413	23,329
15		1,200,515	198,085	0.1229	24,344
16		1,440,618	237,702	0.1069	25,402
17		1,728,742	285,242	0.0929	26,506
18		2,074,490	342,291	0.0808	27,659
19		2,489,388	410,749	0.0703	28,861
20		2,987,266	492,899	0.0611	30,116
			Total PV of	future profits	414,227
				EV	187,880
				AV	602,107
				share price	419.44

Amounts in millions except share price in actuals
PV is the present value
EV is the embedded value on March 31, 2018 (ICICI Pru annual report 2017-2018)
AV is the calculated appraisal value on March 31, 2018

4.5.4. For a base APE of 77,920 million, with a 20 percent increase each year and the NBM at 16.5 percent, the share price works out to Rs 419.44.

4.5.5. If we change the increase in APE to 25 percent, other assumptions remaining the same, the estimated share price becomes Rs 612.24.

SBI Life

NBM = 16.2 percent

VNB = 13.85 (in billions) or 13,850 (in millions)

APE = 85,380 (in millions)

NBM, VNB and APE figures are from SBI Life annual report 2017-2018 (Table 4.3).

Table 4.3 Calculation of SBI Life share price on March 31, 2018

Year	APE Base year	Percentage inc in premium 20%	Profit = NBM @ 16.2% * APE	Disc factor @ 15%	Present value of profit in each year
1	85380	102,456	16,598	0.8696	14,433
2		122,947	19,917	0.7561	15,060
3		147,537	23,901	0.6575	15,715
4		177,044	28,681	0.5718	16,399
5		212,453	34,417	0.4972	17,112
6		254,943	41,301	0.4323	17,855
7		305,932	49,561	0.3759	18,632
8		367,118	59,473	0.3269	19,442
9		440,542	71,368	0.2843	20,287
10		528,650	85,641	0.2472	21,169
11		634,381	102,770	0.2149	22,090
12		761,257	123,324	0.1869	23,050
13		913,508	147,988	0.1625	24,052
14		1,096,210	177,586	0.1413	25,098

(continued)

Table 4.3 Calculation of SBI Life share price on March 31, 2018 (Continued)

Year	APE Base year	Percentage inc in premium 20%	Profit = NBM @ 16.2% * APE	Disc factor @ 15%	Present value of profit in each year
15		1,315,452	213,103	0.1229	26,189
16		1,578,542	255,724	0.1069	27,328
17		1,894,250	306,869	0.0929	28,516
18		2,273,100	368,242	0.0808	29,756
19		2,727,720	441,891	0.0703	31,050
20		3,273,264	530,269	0.0611	32,400
			Total PV of	future profits	445,632
				EV	190,700
				AV	636,332
				share price	636.33

Amounts in millions except share price in actuals
PV is the present value
EV is the embedded value on March 31, 2018 (SBI Life annual report 2017-2018)
AV is the calculated appraisal value on March 31, 2018

4.5.6. Share price is Rs 636.33, assuming a 20 percent increase in APE, 16.2 percent NBM, and a 15 percent discount rate.

4.5.7. If we assume 25 percent growth in APE, all other assumptions remaining the same, the price works out to Rs 934.08.

4.6. I have summarized the results in Table 4.4.

Table 4.4 Summary of calculated share prices

	APE	NBM	VNB	Growth %	Discount rate	Share price
HDFC Life	55,250	23.2%	12,820	20%	15%	280.95
HDFC Life				25%	15%	418.13
ICICI Pru	77,920	16.5%	12,860	20%	15%	419.44
ICICI Pru				25%	15%	612.24
SBI Life	85,380	16.2%	13,850	20%	15%	636.33
SBI Life				25%	15%	934.08

Amounts in millions except share price in actuals

4.6.1. We have calculated the share price assuming growth rates of 20 percent and 25 percent to the APE. Here again we need a benchmark to compare these growth rates. The past experience of these companies will give us a very good idea of what we can expect in the near future.

4.6.2. Table 4.5 gives the past growth in the APE for the last three years.

Table 4.5 Growth in HDFC Life APE

	APE (millions)	Percentage growth
2015	31,945	
2016	37,095	16.12%
2017	41,944	13.07%
2018	55,259	31.74%

The APE figures for 2015 and 2016 were taken from the red herring prospectus in Securities and Exchange Board of India's (SEBI) website. These do not include rural policies, so they are understated, but this is the only information available. 2017 and 2018 APE figures are from the annual reports of those years (Tables 4.6 and 4.7).

Table 4.6 Growth in ICICI Pru APE

	APE(millions)	Percentage growth
2015	47,440	
2016	51,700	8.97%
2017	66,250	28.14%
2018	77,920	17.61%

All APE figures are from 2015, 2016, 2017 and 2018 annual reports of ICICI Pru

Table 4.7 Growth in SBI Life APE

	APE(millions)	Percentage growth
2015	36,060	
2016	50,450	39.91%
2017	67,270	33.33%
2018	85,380	26.92%

All APE figures are from 2018 annual report of SBI Life

4.6.3. We can see that the rates fluctuate wildly from year to year. The investor can put in her assumptions in the model and determine what happens if the growth targets are not met.

4.7. Another important point to note is that the NBM is what the company expects to make in the future. We cannot be sure that the company will be able to achieve this because the contracts run many years into the future and there is no data that proves that the company has, in fact, achieved what it set out to do. Companies generally are very optimistic about their own future performances. Having said this, it is prudent to cut this number by, say, 10 percent so that there is some margin in our calculations.

4.8. This method of calculation, although not very accurate, will give the investor a range for the share price that she is willing to pay. She can also modify the table to
   a. Increase the number of years
   b. Assume a different discount rate
   c. Assume a different NBM
   d. Assume different growth rates for different years as opposed to a constant one for all years

Are these results in any way connected to the price earnings ratio (PER)?

4.9. The aforementioned calculations, in an indirect way, provide a reasoning for the PER. PER varies from industry to industry and also from one company to another in the same industry. A very high PER is a matter of concern, and the investor will do well to keep this information at the back of her mind. A high PER also means that the growth expected in the company is huge and the market places a very high reliance on the future growth prospects.

Conclusion

4.10. We have looked at what the market expects from the companies in the future. We will see in Chapters 5, 6, and 7 how the companies have performed in the recent past by looking at the cash flows.

CHAPTER 5

Cash Flows of the Company

Introduction

5.1. In this chapter, we will first look at the advantages of using the Receipts and Payments Account (Cash Flow statement) over the Revenue Account and try to reconcile the Cash Flow statement to the Revenue Account and the Balance Sheet. We will use the consolidated accounts figures for our analysis.

What are the advantages of using the Cash Flow Statement over the Revenue Account?

5.2. You may ask, why not just use the Revenue Account and the Balance Sheet? Why bother with the Cash Flow statement at all? These questions bring us back to the basics of accounting.

5.3. The Cash Flow statement, Revenue Account, and the Balance Sheet must dovetail each other. Given the Revenue Account and the Balance Sheet, we should be able to chalk out the Cash Flow statement or vice versa. Any basic accounting book will tell us that they are just different angles of the same picture. To appreciate and understand this picture, we need to compare and contrast both the angles and figure out where the differences arise. If we are able to pinpoint the differences, our picture gets clearer, and consequently, our decisions will be more balanced.

5.4. The Cash Flow statement, however, has one very big advantage over the Revenue Account. It is completely inflexible. The company has to record cash transactions as and when they happen and then present them in a particular format. It cannot touch any of the figures in the document. The Revenue Account, on the other hand, has many areas that are left to the discretion of the accountant or the actuary. We may also say that the Cash Flow statement is the unpolished version and the Revenue Account is the dressed version. Since this unpolished version is available, however, we must make full use of it. In many ways, the Cash Flow statement will throw out red flags that the Revenue Account and Balance Sheet may well miss. Many accounting frauds would have come to light much earlier if only the analysts had looked at the Cash Flow statement first. The Cash Flow statement should, therefore, always be our first port of call.

5.5. Ideally, the Cash Flow statement must be looked at independently and analyzed. This method works in almost all industries except insurance, where reserves are set up to meet future liabilities from premiums paid in the past. So the analysis done here is based on a combination of the Cash Flow statement and the reserves from the Revenue Account.

5.6. The companies themselves must look at these figures first when they analyze their own experience. If any problems are spotted, they can be rectified. The problems may remain hidden if the analysts look only at the Revenue Accounts and Balance Sheets.

What does the Cash Flow Statement look like?

5.7. In India, insurance companies follow the direct cash flow method and the results are summarized in the Receipts and Payments Account. A typical Receipts and Payments Account has three sections: cash flow from operating activities, cash flow from investing activities, and cash flow from financing activities. The account heads are as follows:

  i. *Cash flow from operating activities*
     1. Premium
     2. Other income
     3. Net payment to the reinsurer
     4. Claims
     5. Commission
     6. Expenses

      7. Staff loans/security deposit

      8. Income tax

      9. Service tax

     10. Other payments

  ii. *Cash flow from investing activities*

      1. Purchase of fixed assets

      2. Sale of fixed assets

      3. Purchase of investments

      4. Purchase of fixed deposits

      5. Investment in subsidiaries

      6. Security deposits

      7. Loans

      8. Loans to policyholders

      9. Sale of investments

     10. Loan repayments

     11. Interest, rent, or dividend

     12. Dividend income

     13. Investment in money market

     14. Expenses of investment

  iii. *Cash flow from financing activities*

      1. Share capital

      2. Share application pending

      3. Share premium

      4. Dividends paid

      5. Dividend distribution tax (sometimes shown separately)

5.8. Finally, the Cash Flow statement sums all of the above, ie the cash flow from operating activities, cash flow from investing activities and the cash flow from financing activities , states the cash at the beginning, cash at the end, and then the increase or decrease in cash.

What do we do with this information?

5.9. We will first try to reconcile this statement with the Revenue Account and the Balance Sheet. Then we will group this information into a template and calculate ratios and analyze the trends in the figures.

Why do we have to reconcile the Cash Flow Statement with the Balance Sheet and the Revenue Account?

5.10. This serves two purposes:

    5.10.1. One, it proves that the Cash Flow statement is another angle of looking at the Revenue Account. Conclusions drawn from the Cash Flow statement are, therefore, valid and provide an unbiased view of the company's performance.

    5.10.2. Two, it acts as a check on the company's accounts and helps the analyst ask questions that will promote further understanding of the company's accounting policies.

How do we reconcile the Cash Flow Statement to the Revenue Account and the Balance Sheet?

5.11. We can either reconcile each and every item in the Revenue Account or the Balance Sheet, such as premiums, claims, commission, operating expenses, to the corresponding item in the Cash Flow statement or do an overall reconciliation that does not split the differences into the major account heads. I tried to reconcile each and every account head in the Revenue Account and the Balance Sheet but was unsuccessful. The values did not match, and I needed more information.

What is the link between the Balance Sheet and the Cash Flow Statement?

5.12. The Balance Sheet is a snapshot of the company at any one point of time. The Balance Sheet figures at the beginning and the end can be seen as pictures of the company at the beginning and the end of the year, respectively. The Cash Flow statement then is what has happened over the year so that the figures in the Balance Sheet move from one point to another. If we take the end year Balance Sheet figures and subtract them from beginning year Balance Sheet figures, this should equal movements seen in the Cash Flow statement in total.

5.13. Fair value change is the unrealized gain on the investments backing the funds and does not affect the Cash Flow statement, so I have removed the fair value change from both sides of the Balance Sheet.

5.14. The link between the Cash Flow statement and the Balance Sheet is the cash arising over the year, which is the same in both the cases. In effect, the cash flow figures move into different account heads in the Balance Sheet to change the beginning year figures into end year figures.

5.15. To explain this further, I have started off with the Balance Sheet figures. Let us try to understand this pictorially. A typical Balance Sheet looks like Table 5.1:

Table 5.1 Balance Sheet format

Liabilities	Assets
Shareholders' reserves	Shareholders' investments
	Policyholders' investments
	Loans
Policyholders' reserves	Fixed assets
	Net current assets − cash
	Net current assets − others
Funds for future appropriation (FFA)	Provisions

5.16. From one year to the next, there will be changes in each of the account heads. The changes in the Balance Sheet will look like Table 5.2:

Table 5.2 Changes in the Balance Sheet account heads over one year

Liabilities	Assets
Increase in shareholders' reserves	Increase in shareholders' investments
	Increase in policyholders' investments
	Increase in loans
Increase in policyholders' reserves	Increase in fixed assets
	Increase in net current assets − cash
	Increase in net current assets − others
Increase in FFA	Less increase in provisions

5.17. These changes in the Balance Sheet must match the Cash Flow statement for the year in total. As explained earlier, the Cash Flow statement does not take fair value into account. The fair value will affect both sides of the Balance Sheet equally and it must be removed from Table 5.2 from both sides as a first step to reconciliation. The new table will look like Table 5.3:

Table 5.3 Changes in the balance sheet account heads less fair value change

Liabilities	Assets
Increase in shareholders' reserves less increase in fair value for shareholders	Increase in shareholders' investments less increase in fair value for shareholders
	Increase in policyholders' investments less increase in fair value for policyholders
	Increase in loans
Increase in policyholders' reserves less increase in fair value for policyholders	Increase in fixed assets
	Increase in net current assets – cash
	Increase in net current assets – others
Increase in FFA	Less increase in provisions

We now have the changes in the Balance Sheet that must match the Cash Flow statement exactly; that is, different parts of the Cash Flow statement must come and sit in the account heads in Table 5.3.

5.18. Before we move ahead, we need to split the Table 5.3 account heads into smaller parts so that it is easier to reconcile the figures. The split format will look like that shown in Table 5.4.

Table 5.4 Split Balance Sheet format

Liabilities	Assets
• Profit after tax (PAT) • Increase in shareholders' reserves less increase in fair value for shareholders less PAT	• Increase in shareholders' investments less increase in fair value for shareholders
• Increase in policyholders' reserves less increase in fair value for policyholders	• Increase in policyholders' investments less increase in fair value for policyholders less increase in money market instruments • Increase in money market instruments

Table 5.4 (Continued)

Liabilities	Assets
• Increase in FFA	• Increase in loans
	• Increase in fixed assets
	• Increase in current assets – cash
	• Increase in net current assets A • Increase in net current assets B • Increase in net current assets C • Increase in net current assets D
	• Less increase in provisions A • Less increase in provisions B

5.19. The major changes are as follows:
   a. PAT is taken out separately from the increase in shareholders' reserves after fair value and the balance is kept separately.
   b. Current assets are split into four different parts:
      1. Increase in net current assets A is the increase in net current assets related to fixed assets.
      2. Increase in net current assets B is the increase in net current assets related to investment income, purchases and sales of investments. It excludes current assets related to unclaimed amounts.
      3. Increase in net current assets C is the increase in net current assets that relates to unclaimed amount, income on unclaimed amount of policyholders, and unclaimed dividend.
      4. Increase in net current assets D is the balance increase in net current assets after taking out fixed assets, investment income, purchases and sales of investments, unclaimed amount, and income on unclaimed amount of policyholders.
   c. Provisions are split into two parts:
      1. Increase in provisions A is the increase in provisions excluding dividends and dividend distribution tax.
      2. Increase in provisions B is the increase in provisions for dividends and dividend distribution tax.
   d. Money market instruments are taken out of the total investments and subsequently added to the increase in current assets

cash to make it compatible with the Cash Flow statement because the increase in cash arising in the Cash Flow statement is inclusive of money market instruments. I have shown money market instruments as part of the policyholders' investments, but they will form a part of the shareholders' investments as well. This distinction is unimportant for our analysis, so it does not matter where the money market instruments are shown, provided they are removed from the investments and shown as part of the increase in current assets cash.

5.20. The left hand side and the right hand side now represent the total increases from one year to the next excluding fair value increases and are in the format we want. We can move every account head on the right hand side of the Balance Sheet to the left hand side, except the increase in net current assets cash and the increase in money market instruments, to form an equation. To do this we have to change the signage of everything that we move from the right hand side to the left hand side.

5.21. The table is now expressed as an equation and the new equation becomes

PAT

plus (increase in shareholders' reserves less increase in fair value for shareholders less PAT)

plus (increase in policyholders' reserves less increase in fair value for policyholders)

plus increase in FFA

less (increase in shareholders' investments less increase in fair value for shareholders)

less (increase in policyholders' investments less increase in fair value for policyholders less increase in money market instruments)

less increase in loans

less increase in fixed assets

less increase in net current assets A

less increase in net current assets B

less increase in net current assets C

less increase in net current assets D

plus increase in provisions A

plus increase in provisions B

Equals

Increase in current assets cash

plus increase in money market instruments

5.22. We will now rearrange the above equation into different groups. The equation becomes

Group 1

PAT

plus increase in provisions A

less increase in net current assets D

plus

Group 2

(Increase in shareholders' reserves less increase in fair value for shareholders less PAT)

plus increase in provisions B

plus

Group 3

$$X - Y$$

Where X =

(Increase in policyholders' reserves less increase in fair value for policyholders)

plus increase in FFA

and Y =

(Increase in shareholders' investments less increase in fair value for shareholders)

plus (increase in policyholders' investments less increase in fair value for policyholders less increase in money market instruments)

plus increase in net current assets B

plus increase in net current assets C

plus

Group 4

— (Increase in fixed assets plus increase in net current assets A)

plus

Group 5

— (Increase in loans)

Equals

Group 6

Increase in current assets cash plus increase in money market instruments

5.23. We will revisit these six groups after we arrange the Cash Flow statement in the format that we want. Before we start, I will explain the signage in the Cash Flow statement.

A note on signage in the Cash Flow Statement

5.24. The Cash Flow statement in its basic form is an equation that starts with the premiums collected, income earned, and so on and then goes on to subtract claims paid, expenses incurred, and so on. Any cash going out of the company, therefore, figures here with a negative sign and any cash coming in has a positive sign. For example, purchases mean that the company uses cash to buy assets, so purchases are negative. By the same argument, sales come here with a positive sign. In our analysis, we are picking up figures from the Cash Flow statement that already have positive or negative signs attached to them and I have left this signage unchanged.

5.25. The Balance Sheet, on the other hand, does not have any signs attached to its numbers. For example, provisions is a liability, but it does not have a negative sign attached to it. The signs have to be put in by the analyst. I have specified this signage in the Balance Sheet numbers, whereas I have left the Cash Flow statement signage unchanged.

5.26. This distinction has to be kept in mind throughout this chapter.

Regrouping the Cash Flow Statement

5.27. As explained earlier, the Cash Flow statement consists of three parts: operating, investing, and financing. The operating and financing parts can be left as is, but the investing part has to be grouped into three parts. The Investing Cash Flow accounting heads can be regrouped as follows:

a. Purchase and sale of fixed assets

b. Purchase and sale of investments; fixed deposits; subsidiaries; security deposits; interest, rent, and dividend; dividend income; money market; and expenses of investment

c. Loan and loan repayments

5.28. The Cash Flow statement can be regrouped and expressed as follows:

Group 1

Operating Cash Flow
plus

Group 2

Financing Cash Flow
plus

Group 3

Purchase and sale of investments; fixed deposits; subsidiaries; security deposits; interest, rent, and dividend; dividend income; money market; and expenses of investment
plus

Group 4

Purchase and sale of fixed assets
plus

Group 5

Loan and loan repayments
Equals

Group 6

Net increase in cash and cash equivalents in the Cash Flow statement

5.29. We now have six groups from the differences in the Balance Sheet table and six groups from the Cash Flow statement.

5.30. Group 6 is the net increase in cash and cash equivalents. This is the same in both the Cash Flow statement and the differences of the Balance Sheet statement. In both the statements, group 1 + group 2 + group 3 + group 4 + group 5 = group 6. Therefore, group 1 + ... + group 5 of the Cash Flow statement must equal group 1 + ... + group 5 of the differences in the Balance Sheet statement.

5.31. In each of the groups, we have a Cash Flow statement figure and a Balance Sheet figure. We will find the differences in each group as Cash Flow statement figure less Balance Sheet figure. We start with Group 1.

Group 1: Reconciliation

Cash Flow Statement

Cash Flow statement figure is the Operating Cash Flow with some adjustments.

Adjusted Cash Flow Figure for the comparison or the calculated PAT from the Cash Flow statement is

Operating Cash Flow
less depreciation
less increase in provisions A

plus investment income for policyholders in the Revenue Account
plus investment income for shareholders in the Revenue Account
plus increase in net current assets D
less increase in policyholders' reserves in the Revenue Account
less increase in FFA

Balance Sheet

Balance Sheet figure is the PAT

Why are we removing or adding all these items to Operating Cash Flow? Can we not just compare PAT with Operating Cash Flow?

5.31.1. The Cash Flow statement deals only with cash spent and cash earned. By its very nature, there are no provisions, reserves, or current assets and current liabilities. Also, investment income figures only in the Investing Cash Flow and has no place in the Operating Cash Flow. To compare like with like, we have to either add what is missing or subtract what is extra. Let us now consider the adjustment items one by one.

a. Depreciation: This is an accounting adjustment to smooth the cost of fixed assets over their life. The Cash Flow statement only records the purchases and sales of fixed assets and they form part of the investing and not Operating Cash Flow. These cash flows are completely different from the depreciation that figures in the Revenue Account. To bring the Operating Cash Flow to the PAT, depreciation should be reduced from the Operating Cash Flow. This figure is a straight lift from schedule 10. In some years, the depreciation in schedules 3, 3A, and 3B do not add up to the depreciation figure in schedule 10. I have ignored this anomaly and used the schedule 10 figure.

b. Increase in provisions: The Cash Flow statement does not deal with provisions, but the Revenue Account does. Sometimes, the provisions may also include provisions for dividend and dividend distribution tax. PAT is unaffected by this as the dividend and dividend distribution tax will be paid only after profits are declared. Therefore, we have to reduce only increase in provision A (which is the provisions excluding dividend and dividend distribution tax) from the Operating Cash Flow.

c. Increase in investment income for both shareholders and policyholders: These figure in the Revenue Account, and in the Cash Flow statement they form part of the Investing Cash Flow. They have, therefore, to be added to the Operating Cash Flow for the reconciliation. The investment income must exclude transfers from the shareholders' to policyholders' account and vice versa. It must also exclude other miscellaneous income and income from unclaimed amount in the policyholders' fund. Other miscellaneous income is excluded because the Operating Cash Flow also has other income as one of its components and these two are assumed to be the same. Please refer to the note on unclaimed amount (section 5.3.2) to understand the reason for excluding it.

d. Increase in net current assets D: Net current assets do not form part of the Cash Flow statement, but are very much present in the Revenue Account. For example, premium in the Cash Flow statement is just premium collected over the year, whereas premium in the Revenue Account is premium accrued over the year. Accrued premium is the premium collected plus the increase in the net current assets for the premium. So, when we are moving from the Cash Flow statement to the Revenue Account, we have to add back the net current assets for each and every item in the Revenue Account. The net current assets, however, cannot be taken as they are because some part of the net current assets relates to fixed assets, investments, and unclaimed amounts. Only net current assets D (which excludes fixed assets, investment income, purchases and sales, and unclaimed amounts) has to be allowed for here and this has to be added to the Operating Cash Flow. We have to exclude the net current assets for the investment income also because investment income from the Revenue Account is added as is, and therefore, does not need to be adjusted. Unclaimed dividends are also excluded for the same reason as unclaimed amounts. In HDFC Life and SBI Life, this is shown as a separate item in the current liability. SBI Life has shown this as zero and ICICI Pru has grouped this with other liabilities. For ICICI Pru, this figure is available for 2018 and 2017 as a footnote in the Cash Flow statement, and I have reduced this amount in 2018 and 2017 from the current liability. I have also assumed that before 2017 there are no current assets especially earmarked for unclaimed amounts, and so, I have not made any adjustments for the same.

e. Increase in reserves and increase in FFA: The Cash Flow statement does not deal with reserves of any kind, but the Revenue Account does. These reserves, therefore, have to be subtracted from the Operating Cash Flow.

5.31.2. The net effect of these adjustments must bring the Operating Cash Flow to the PAT.

5.31.3. In Group 1 reconciliation, we introduced extra items to the Operating Cash Flow that now have to be added to other groups on the Balance Sheet side so that the total is not disturbed. These are depreciation (which will now be added to Group 4 Balance Sheet), increase in reserves, increase in FFA and investment income for both the shareholders and the policyholders. These will now form part of Group 3 Balance Sheet and the sum of all of these (except depreciation) is called Z. Increase in net current assets D and increase in provisions A will now be added to balance sheet group 1. Since balance sheet group 1 already has these two items with exactly the opposite sign, they will cancel each other out and we will be left with only the PAT. The balance sheet figure will therefore be only the PAT.

Group 2: Reconciliation

Cash Flow Statement

Financing Cash Flow is the sum of share capital, share premiums, share application pending, dividends paid, and the dividend distribution tax. Forex also forms part of this in some companies and so forex is dealt with case by case.

Balance Sheet

Balance Sheet financing figure is the
(Increase in shareholders' reserves less increase in fair value for shareholders less PAT) plus increase in provisions B

Group 3: Reconciliation

Cash Flow Statement

Cash flow investing figure is the sum of purchase and sale of investments; fixed deposits; subsidiaries; security deposits; interest, rent, and dividend; dividend income; money market; and expenses of investment

Balance Sheet

Balance Sheet investing figure is the sum of $X - Y + Z$ where
$X =$ (Increase in policyholders' reserves less increase in fair value for policyholders)
plus increase in FFA

Y = (Increase in shareholders' investments less increase in fair value for shareholders)

plus (Increase in policyholders' investments less increase in fair value for policyholders)

less increase in money market instruments

plus increase in net current assets B

plus increase in net current assets C

and

Z = Investment income for policyholders in the Revenue Account

plus investment income for shareholders in the Revenue Account

less increase in policyholders' reserves in the Revenue Account

(This figure is a straight lift from the Revenue Account and it includes fair value that comes through the Revenue Account. This is different from the increase in reserves calculated in X, which removes the effect of the fair value increase.)

less increase in FFA

5.31.4. Z is what has been added in Group 1 reconciliation to the Operating Cash Flow, except for depreciation, increase in net current assets D and increase in provisions A.

Group 4: Reconciliation

Cash Flow Statement

Cash flow fixed assets = Purchase and sale of fixed assets

Balance Sheet

Balance Sheet fixed assets = − (Increase in fixed assets plus increase in net current assets A plus depreciation)

Please refer to Groups 1 and 3 reconciliation for the explanation.

Group 5: Reconciliation

Cash Flow Statement

Cash flow loan = Loan and loan repayments

Balance Sheet

Balance Sheet loans $= -$ Increase in loans

Group 6: Reconciliation

Cash Flow Statement

Cash arising over the year in the Cash Flow statement

Balance Sheet

Increase in cash plus increase in money market instruments

5.31.5. This we know is equal.

Note on unclaimed amount of policyholders and income on unclaimed amount

5.32. From April 1, 2016, companies have to hold current assets earmarked for unclaimed amounts and income on unclaimed amounts.

    5.32.1. Unclaimed amounts are those for which cheques have been issued but the policyholders have not encashed them. This means that both the Cash Flow statement and the Revenue Account have already registered these as claims. Consequently, this does not need any special adjustment while reconciling in Group 1.

    5.32.2. Income on unclaimed amounts will be part of the investment income and the claims in the Revenue Account in the year in which they are earned. They will not touch the Cash Flow statement at all. In the event of a claim, current assets that have been set up will be reduced to meet this liability.

    5.32.3. I have, therefore, ignored this in computing net current assets D, both in the current assets (where it figures after a change in regulations in 2017) and in current liabilities (where it figures in all the years).

PHEW!!!!

5.33. Finally, the sum of all the differences between the five groups must equal? You guessed it, *zero*.

Do we always get a zero if the reconciliation is done in this way?

5.34. The answer is *no*.

    5.34.1. Sometimes, the accounting numbers change from one year to the next. For example, the accounting numbers of the previous year in the current year's accounts are very different from those in the annual report of the previous year. This means that you are looking at two different sets of numbers.

    5.34.2. To avoid this problem, you must pick figures only from one year's annual report even if they are different from the annual report of the previous year. This will ensure that you are looking at numbers that are consistent with each other. If you do this, the answer must equal zero or come very close to zero after allowing for rounding errors.

5.35. As an example, I have done the reconciliation for SBI Life for 2017 and HDFC Life for 2018.

SBI Life and HDFC Life reconciliation of Cash Flow Statement with Balance Sheet

5.36. The differences calculated for each group are always Cash Flow statement numbers less Balance Sheet numbers.

    5.36.1. Signage in the Cash Flow statement figures is a straight lift from the Cash Flow statement and is left unchanged.

    5.36.2. Signage for the Balance Sheet numbers and the adjustments is what has been mentioned in the table (Tables 5.5–5.9).

    5.36.3. Amounts are in thousands.

Table 5.5 SBI Life and HDFC Life Group 1 reconciliation

	SBI Life 2016–2017	HDFC Life 2017–2018
Cash flow		
Operating Cash Flow	85,251,158	67,392,824
less depreciation	475,586	447,087
less increase in provisions A	122,182	−27,349
plus policyholders' investment income	92,949,841	85,946,319
plus shareholders' investment income	4,015,594	2,841,224
plus increase in net current assets D	−352,142	−8,078,521
less increase in policyholders' reserves	172,409,642	133,222,515
less increase in FFA	0	924,134
Cash flow PAT	8,857,041	13,535,459
Balance Sheet		
Balance Sheet PAT	9,546,529	11,072,030
Difference for Group 1	−689,488	2,463,429

Table 5.6 SBI Life and HDFC Life Group 2 reconciliation

	SBI Life 2016–2017	HDFC Life 2017–2018
Cash flow		
Cash flow financing figure	−1,444,292	−1,961,075
Balance Sheet		
Shareholders' reserves at year end less fair value	54,647,810	47,051,039
less shareholders' reserves at year beginning less fair value	46,906,647	37,940,088
less PAT	9,546,529	11,072,030
plus increase in provisions B	361,073	0
Balance Sheet financing figure	−1,444,293	−1,961,079
Difference for Group 2	1	4

Table 5.7 SBI Life and HDFC Life Group 3 reconciliation

	SBI Life 2016–2017	HDFC Life 2017–2018
Cash flow		
Purchase of Investments	−749,287,537	−606,292,470
Money market	+2,190,314	−4,934
Sale of investments	+610,555,283	+514,827,959
Interest, rent, dividends	+45,738,772	+47,304,143

Table 5.7 (*Continued*)

	SBI Life 2016–2017	HDFC Life 2017–2018
Dividend income	+2,590,165	0
Expenses of investments	−72,384	−9,238
Cash flow investing	−88,285,387	−44,174,540
Balance Sheet		
X		
Policyholders' reserves at year end less fair value	891,066,286	914,822,670
less policyholders' reserves at year beginning less fair value	733,857,245	784,056,913
plus FFA at year end	0	9,591,963
less FFA at year beginning	2,306	8,667,828
Sum of X	157,206,735	131,689,892
Y		
Shareholders' investments at year end less fair value	42,082,068	40,271,944
less shareholders' investments at year beginning less fair value	35,224,660	31,990,996
plus policyholders' investments at year end less fair value	869,682,397	938,772,150
less policyholders' investments at year beginning less fair value	716,722,806	803,163,824
less money market investments at year end	7,271,245	56,930,670
plus money market investments at year beginning	11,912,821	38,841,578
plus net current assets B at year end	17,815,404	6,091,196
less net current assets B at year beginning	17,972,302	3,850,811
plus net current assets C at year end	0	−1,700
Less net current assets C at year beginning	−6,533,770	−187
Sum of Y	170,835,447	128,039,054
Z		
Investment income of shareholders	4,015,594	2,841,224
plus investment income of policyholders	92,949,841	85,946,319
less increase in policyholders' reserves	172,409,642	133,222,515
less increase in FFA	0	924,134
Sum of Z	−75,444,207	−45,359,106
Balance Sheet investing figure = Sum of X − Y + Z	−89,072,219	−41,708,268
Difference for Group 3	787,532	−2,466,272

Table 5.8 SBI Life and HDFC Life Group 4 reconciliation

	SBI Life 2016–2017	HDFC Life 2017–2018
Cash Flow		
Fixed assets		
Purchases	−1,484,672	−338,771
Sales	+2,867	10,687
Cash flow fixed assets	−1,481,805	−328,084
Balance Sheet		
Minus year end fixed assets	5,384,749	3,416,942
plus year beginning fixed assets	4,472,485	3,534,652
Minus year end net current assets A	0	11,640
plus year beginning net currents assets A	0	10,094
less depreciation	475,586	447,087
Balance Sheet fixed assets	−1,387,850	−330,923
Difference for Group 4	−93,955	2,839

Table 5.9 SBI Life and HDFC Life Group 5 reconciliation

	SBI Life 2016–2017	HDFC Life 2017–2018
Cash flow		
Loans	−745,214	−72,388
Repayments	+200,000	363,513
Cash flow loans	−545,214	291,125
Balance Sheet		
Minus year end loans	1,781,994	187,391
plus year beginning loans	1,235,623	478,516
Balance Sheet loans	−546,371	291,125
Difference for Group 5	+1,157	0

Forex

This forms part of the shareholders' share of reserves but is missing in the balance sheet for SBI Life. It is, however, present in the cash flow statement. So, it will be taken as is at −5,245.

Net differences

This is the sum of all the differences in the groups plus the forex difference.

	SBI Life 2016–2017	HDFC Life 2017–2018
Group 1	−689,488	2,463,429
Group 2	1	4
Group 3	787,532	−2,466,272
Group 4	−93,955	2,839
Group 5	1,157	0
Forex	−5,245	Included in Group 2
Total	2	0

5.37. The ideal answer should be zero, but I think 2 is something we can live with.

Why is there such a big difference in each of the groups? Should not there be a zero in each of the rows above?

5.38. Zero in each of the rows above is the ideal scenario we aim for. This means that the Cash Flow statement exactly dovetails the Revenue Account and the Balance Sheet. This generally does not happen even when the companies follow the most meticulous accounting procedures. For example, the Group 4 reconciliation in HDFC Life has a positive 2,839 figure, which is just the difference in the fixed assets. This positive has to be offset by another negative elsewhere in another group because the total of the differences will always be zero, no matter what. This means that the reconciliation of another group will take a hit.

5.39. It could also mean that I have missed out some item that should be added to that group or added another item that should not be there. Group 1 and Group 3 in HDFC Life are good examples to use to demonstrate this point. The differences are significant and we need to work that issue out with the accounts department to whittle it down some more.

After the reconciliation, what do we do now?

5.40. Now that the reconciliation is out of the way and we are sure that the Cash Flow statement is just another angle of the published accounts, we can use the data in the Cash Flow statement for our analysis. The next chapter speaks about how to analyze the data in the Cash Flow statement.

CHAPTER 6

Analysis of the Cash Flow Statement: A New Format

Introduction

6.1. To analyze the three companies we will first look at a few ratios we need and then explain how to change the Group 1 reconciliation format so that we may compare different companies and different years of the same company. This chapter will build the framework for our analysis.

Which ratios do we calculate, and what are we looking for?

6.2. We will calculate the following ratios for all the three companies. The calculations are done in chapter 7; here I will explain how to calculate the ratios and also how to draw conclusions from them.

6.2.1. Commission/premium

The lower the percentage, the better it is for the profitability of the company. A lower percentage may, however, make the sales force unhappy and demotivated, and the company may be able to increase profitability by paying a higher commission and targeting a different market segment, increasing the minimum policy size, trying a different sales channel or selling a different product. The trick is to strike the right balance—easier said than done!

6.2.2. Percentage increase in premium

Higher the percentage, more is the business written. This may not always be good, however, because the business may be unprofitable, or worse, loss making.

6.2.3. Claims/premium

6.2.3.1. Claims experience is extremely important, but it is almost impossible for us to analyze the claims experience because we do not have all the information that we need to comment accurately. We can, therefore, only guess and hope that the ratios will throw out red flags. Claims experience has also been erratic, and it is difficult to say what the effect on the profitability is. The negative of a high benefit ratio is that money goes off the books.

6.2.3.2. This does not mean, however, that the company always makes a loss in its benefits payments. Surrenders carry penalties, and if the contract has been on the company's books for a long time, the company ensures that it does not lose out, provided the regulations allow the company to do so. If the benefit paid is less than what the company holds in respect of that one policy, it is profitable for the company, and vice versa.

6.2.3.3. Even for those benefit payments where the company has made a profit, if the company could have made more profits had the contract remained in its books, there is a loss. This can be calculated only if we have access to all the company records. Most companies undertake this exercise on an ongoing basis, although these results are not made public.

6.2.4. Percentage increase in operating expenses

If the premiums increase, it is natural to expect an increase in the operating expenses because operating expenses are impacted by the number of new policies sold. An increase in premium is always accompanied by an increase in the number of new policies on the company's books. This ratio gives us an idea of how the current year's expenses compare with those of the previous year.

6.2.5.   Operating expenses/premium

The comments here are the same as for commission.

Is there anything else we can do with this Group 1 reconciliation?

6.3. The previous chapter shows the reconciliation for one year for two companies and these are just examples to show how the reconciliation works. Now, I have done the reconciliation for all the three companies for seven years from 2012 to 2018 in chapter 7.

6.4. This helps us identify the years in which the calculated PAT is markedly different from the Revenue Account PAT. The analyst then needs to identify those years and ask the accounts department whether there were any changes in the accounting policies in those particular years. We can put this reconciliation to good use by tweaking it slightly and changing the presentation in such a way that it helps us analyze the data better. This will not only help us in judging how one company has fared in different years of operation but will also help us in gauging the performance of one company against another. This is a three-step process:

a. The first step is to split the Operating Cash Flow into premiums, other income, claims, commission, operating expenses, staff loans, income tax, and service tax. These items along with the adjustments for reconciliation are then put together as follows:

Premium (excluding net payment to the reinsurer) plus other income less claims less expenses

plus (shareholders' investment income plus policyholders' investment income less increase in reserves [excluding reduction in reserves for reinsurance])

plus net payment to the reinsurer

plus reduction in reserves for reinsurance

less increase in FFA par

less increase in FFA non-par

less income tax

less service tax

plus advances, loans, and other deposits

less depreciation

less increase in provisions A

plus increase in net current assets D

Equals

Cash flow PAT

     b. The second step is to introduce net current assets B—the net current assets for investment income, purchases, and sales—into this reconciliation. We have to both add and subtract this so that the equation is not disturbed. This is first subtracted from the investment income and then added after the increase in net current assets D.

     c. The third step is to introduce Cash Margin, Cash before Tax and Cash for Shareholders. I will explain these as we go along.

6.5. The revised reconciliation format then becomes as follows:

Premium (excluding net payment to reinsurer) plus other income less claims less expenses

plus (investment income [shareholders plus policyholders] less increase in reserves [excluding reinsurance] less increase in net current assets B)

Equals Cash Margin

plus net payment to reinsurer

plus reduction in reserves due to reinsurance

less increase in FFA par

less increase in FFA non-par

Equals Cash before Tax

less income tax

less service tax

plus advances, loans, and deposits

Equals Cash for Shareholders

less depreciation

less increase in provisions A

plus increase in net current assets D

plus increase in net current assets B

Equals Cash Flow PAT

6.6. We will call this Group 1 detailed reconciliation in the following chapter.

Why are we subtracting Net Current Assets B from the Investment Income?

6.7. We need a Cash Flow statement equivalent to investment income less increase in reserves. By subtracting the increase in net current assets B from the investment income (which is taken from the Revenue Account) and the increase in reserves, we arrive at a Cash Flow statement estimate consistent with the other items like premium, claims, and expenses. To ensure equality, we have to add this back again so that the final result, that is, the PAT calculated from the Cash Flow statement, remains the same.

What do the Cash Margin, Cash before Tax, and the Cash for Shareholders mean?

6.8. Cash Margin is what is left over from the premiums after the company has met its claims and expenses and also reserved for its liabilities. Reinsurance reserves, reinsurance claims, and reinsurance premiums are, however, excluded in this calculation.

6.9. Cash before Tax shows the added effect to Cash Margin of reinsurance and the contribution to or the withdrawal from the FFA.

6.10. Finally, the Cash for Shareholders shows what is left over after all the liabilities are met. This can also be viewed as the base on which the PAT is built. All of these measures can be used to compare one company against another and also different years of the same company.

6.11. The check for us is the final row in Group 1 detailed reconciliation table , which is the difference in calculated PAT and Revenue Account PAT. This should remain the same in both Group 1 reconciliation table and Group 1 detailed reconciliation table. This row tells us that both the tables are the same and that Group 1 detailed reconciliation table is only presented in a different way to help us analyze the company better.

What are we looking for in the new format?

6.12. We will now analyze the trends in the groups in the restated format.

6.12.1. Premium less claims less expenses: This is often flaunted in the annual report and accounts if it makes the company look good and ignored if it shows the company in a bad light. This is the extra money the company has each year after it meets its most important outgo. An increase in this figure signifies that the company is growing. If this stagnates or reduces, it may mean that the company is not growing as expected, or the claims and expenses are too high.

6.12.2. Investment income (both shareholders' and policyholders') less increase in reserves (excluding reinsurance): This is the net amount of money the company has to invest to meet its obligations to the policyholders. Reserves here do not take into account the reduction due to reinsurance.

6.12.3. Cash Margin: This is a very important part of the analysis and is explained in detail in the next section.

6.12.4. Net payment to the reinsurer: This is the net of reinsurance premium, reinsurance claims and reinsurance commission. This is the company's outgo to the reinsurer. This can also be seen as the cost of reinsurance.

6.12.5. Reduction in reserves because of reinsurance: This gives the amount of reduced reserves the company holds because of its reinsurance arrangements. Generally, this forms part of the reserves and is not highlighted separately. Because of the huge differences between the companies and also between different years of the same company, I have brought it out separately. The more the reduction, the more is the increase in the PAT.

6.12.6. Increase in FFA: This is the amount set aside out of the surplus arising each year and can be used in the future to add to the surplus on the basis of the actuary's recommendation. Companies are not mandated to set aside this amount, and it is discretionary. If this value is negative, money is drawn out of the fund and used to augment the surplus arising in the year.

I have split this further into FFA par and FFA non-par. Sometimes in the Balance Sheet it is expressed as a split between linked and non-linked business, although a better split would be par and non-par. This is because the non-linked business can be either par or non-par and this will affect the FFA split between shareholders and policyholders.

a. FFA par: If FFA par is positive, it will be shared between the shareholders and the policyholders in the future, where 90 percent of this will go to the policyholders and 10 percent to the shareholders. If this is negative, the policyholders receive the surplus in the form of bonus, which will amount to 90 percent of FFA, and only 10 percent is given to the shareholders.

b. FFA non-par: Since it is FFA in the non-par fund, it is fully credited to the shareholders' account.

c. The split of the FFA into or from the different funds is available in the segmental Revenue Account. It is not uniform across funds and in the same year there can be both a positive value in one fund and a negative value in another.

6.12.7. Cash before Tax: This is the balance amount the company has from the Cash Margin after the payment to the reinsurer, addition of the reinsurance reserves and the FFA contribution.

6.12.8. Income tax: This is just to compare and contrast the taxes paid by each company because taxes have a direct relationship with the performance of the company.

6.12.9. Service Tax: Same as the previous explanation.

6.12.10. Advances and loans: This is the net amount of loans or advances given.

6.12.11. Cash for Shareholders: This is the amount the company has after it has met all its obligations, including taxation and capital expenses. It is, therefore, the amount the company has before it pays any dividends or makes any adjustments to calculate the Revenue Account numbers. Cash available can also be seen as the profit after tax before the effect of the current assets, provisions, and depreciation but after reserves, reinsurance, and taxation. It is a bit like looking at the base values on which the Revenue Account is built.

6.12.12.   Cash flow PAT: In an ideal scenario, this has to equal the Revenue Account PAT. Minor differences can be overlooked but major differences have to be understood by obtaining more information from the company's accounts department.

6.12.13.   Before we move ahead, I would like to define two terms, new business strain and profit signature.

What is new business strain and profit signature?

6.13.   Let us consider every item in the Cash Margin only for new business and try to get an estimate of what we expect it to be at the end of the year.

6.13.1.   Claims for new business are usually negligible in the first year and so we give this a zero value.

6.13.2.   Expenses can be split into commission and operating expenses.

6.13.2.1.   Let us assume that the company pays 10 percent commission for new business. Generally speaking, commission for new business is more than the commission for renewal business.

6.13.2.2.   Here, I would like to digress and comment on the commission rates. To get an idea of what these rates in the three companies are, we can use schedule 1 and schedule 2 of the annual reports and accounts to calculate them. The rates for the three companies are as given in Table 6.1.

Table 6.1 First year and renewal commission rates for HDFC Life,
ICICI Pru and SBI Life

	HDFC Life			ICICI Pru			SBI Life		
	2018	2017	2016	2018	2017	2016	2018	2017	2016
FY COMM %	18.37%	18.11%	17.45%	13.93%	7.25%	7.60%	8.66%	8.15%	10.33%
REN COMM %	1.27%	1.28%	1.25%	1.93%	2.00%	1.94%	2.74%	2.45%	2.53%

6.13.2.3. A quick note on the commission here. ICICI Pru has a sudden jump in commission in 2018, but despite this jump, the commission is lower than the HDFC Life commission. If this increased expenditure results in higher profits, it is justified—but this remains to be seen.

6.13.2.4. Coming back to our example, a very high percentage of the operating expenses relate to the capture of new business. This break up is not available in the accounts, but if we apportion everything between new and renewal business, we will not be surprised to find that new business expenses account for about 50 percent of the total operating expenses, and in terms of the new business premium collected, may account for around 20 percent.

6.13.3. Reserves built for the new business depend on the product design and may sometimes be 80 percent of the premium in linked businesses.

6.13.4. We now have claims, commission, operating expenses, and reserves in terms of the premium collected.

6.13.5. Putting all this in premium less claims less expenses (both commission and operating) less increase in reserves, we get

Premium	Premium
Less claims	Less zero
Less commission	Less 10% × premium
Less operating expenses	Less 20% of premium
Less increase in reserves	Less 80% of premium
equals	−10% of premium

6.14. This means that the company has to spend 10 percent of the premium in the first year to get this new business on its books. This is called *new business strain* and has the effect of depressing profits in the very first year of operation. The company more than makes up for this in the later years, and this negative in the first year is followed by many positives in future years. This sequence of cash flows for all the policy years is called the *profit signature*. This is best explained with an example.

6.15. Let us assume that the company writes only one product, and the cash flow for one policy is as follows.

  6.15.1. For the purpose of this exercise, we will ignore surrenders, deaths, interest earned, reinsurance and taxation. The premium is assumed to be 100.

Year	1	2	3	4	5
	−10	5	5	6	7

  6.15.2. The cash flow in the first year is the extra the company pays from its pocket, and the cash flow in the later years is the profit it earns each year. The profit the company hopes to make in this one policy is $-10 + 5 + 5 + 6 + 7 = 13$. The new business strain is, therefore, 10 and the profit is 13, which makes the new business margin (NBM) $= 13/100 = 13$ percent.

  6.15.3. For the same NBM of 13 percent, you can have an entirely different set of cash flows, for example,

Year	1	2	3	4	5
	1	2	3	3	4

In this example, there is no new business strain, instead, a profit of 1 comes through in year 1. It is possible to design products that have no new business strain. Again, that depends on the products of the competitors, regulatory requirements, and so on.

6.15.4. The sequence of cash flows is called the profit signature of the contract. For the same NBM, we can have many different profit signatures as the profit signature is a combination of the amount of profits released in each future year and the new business strain of the contract.

6.16. The embedded value of the contract at the time of writing the policy is 13 and this will form part of the value of new business written in the year.

6.17. One year down the line, if everything is as expected,

6.17.1. we would have had a negative cash flow of 10, which will form part of the adjusted net worth (ANW), and we would expect to get 5 now and 5+6+7= 18 in the future.

6.17.2. The value of in force (VIF) now becomes 18; the ANW before this year's cash flow is −10, and the current year's cash flow is 5, keeping the embedded value unchanged at 13.

6.17.3. For a single contract, therefore, if the experience is exactly as expected, the balance between the ANW and the VIF keeps changing from year to year, the embedded value remaining the same.

6.17.4. In practice, everything is variable, as our experience will not be as expected and we will also revise our assumptions of the future.

What is the relationship between new business strain, profit signature, cash margin and embedded value?

6.18. Let us assume now that the company has written seven policies in the first year and is in the fourth year of operation. The cash flow of the company will now look like this.

6.18.1. Cash flow of the policies written in the first year:

Year	4	5
Profit	7×6 = 42	7×7=49

6.18.2. In addition to this existing business the company now writes two new policies. Cash flow of the two new policies will be

year	4	5	6	7	8
	−20	10	10	12	14

6.18.3. The sum of the two cash flows will be

year	4	5	6	7	8
	22	59	10	12	14

6.18.4. This cash flow of 22 is what is defined as our Cash Margin. (This is because in this example, there is no reinsurance or taxation. Cash Margin should be replaced with Cash for Shareholders to allow for reinsurance and taxation.)

6.18.4.1. This is the sum of our experience in the policies written previously and also the new business strain written in the current year.

6.18.4.2. The present value of all these Cash Margins will be the total profitability of the business written till date and is also called the *value of in-force policies*. VIF in the above example is 59+10+12+14 = 95.

6.18.4.3. The sum of the Cash Margin, VIF, and ANW is 22+ 95 + 0= 117, which is also the embedded value of one contract × number of contracts = 13× 9.

6.18.4.4. ANW is zero, because the cash flows until time 3 is −10× 7 + 5×7 + 5×7= 0

6.19. Since the Cash Margin becomes part of the embedded value at the end of the year, factors affecting the Cash Margin will also affect the embedded value of the company. These are as follows:

6.19.1. The size of the business written

If companies write more business, their new business strain will increase, thereby reducing the Cash Margin.

6.19.2. The mix of business

Some products are more profitable than others. A higher percentage of these products will increase the Cash Margin.

6.19.3. Experience of the existing business in the year

The cash flow of the existing business depends on the experience in the current year. In particular, it depends on the claims, expenses, and the investment income earned over the year.

6.19.4. The distribution channel

The distribution channel has a direct impact on expenses, especially those incurred in the very first policy year. It also has a secondary impact on the claims and surrender experience as it will affect the quality of business.

6.19.5. Strength of reserves

6.19.5.1. Reserves will affect the amount the company holds with respect to one contract. If the reserves are strong, the company holds more money and this will affect the profit signature of the contract.

6.19.5.2. Please note that reserves affect only the timing and not the actual profits earned on the contract. This means that the profits will be released later than earlier in the duration of the contract. This will reduce the VIF because profits are discounted for a longer time period, and this will impact our profitability.

What does the Cash Margin say then?

6.20.   To understand the Cash Margin, we have to split it into many components and analyze the impact of each. It is impossible to do this with just published information. For example, a low cash margin could be low premiums, poor claims, high expenses, poor investment income, strong reserves, or high new business strain. Low premium growth, and poor investment performance are definitely bad for the company. Poor claims and high expenses again may be bad depending on the circumstances. High new business strain is good if the business written is profitable and the strength of the reserves will only have a small impact. So, overall, it is very difficult to comment on the profitability of the company on the basis of only this value. The Cash Margin, however, has two very important functions.

6.20.1.   The companies we are looking into are almost in the same phase of growth, are competing in the same market, and have written premiums that are very close to each other. Having said this, it is reasonable to assume that they should not be too far out of line with each other. If we find any year's cash margin too different from either the previous years' figures or another company's figure for the same year, it is reason enough to explore further.

6.20.2.   The VIF of the company is the present value of the Cash Margin of the future years of the company after allowing for the following:

a.   Reduction in reserves for reinsurance

b.   Taxation

c.   Advances, loans

d.   Depreciation

6.20.2.1.   The net effect of reinsurance on the profits of the company is the cost of reinsurance. Whether reinsurance is material or not depends on how this cost compares with the profits of the company. It can be either a positive or a negative. Either way, it should only have a minimal impact unless the terms of the reinsurance company are totally different from what is expected.

6.20.2.2. The only material element here is taxation. Strictly speaking, the VIF should also allow for the cost of capital, options , guarantees and residual risks. These may reduce the VIF by about 5%. I am ignoring these for now to concentrate on the big picture.

6.20.2.3. We will look at reinsurance and taxation in more detail in the next chapter.

6.20.3. Effectively, the VIF can then be considered as Cash Margin for each future year less tax, discounted to the present date. The current year's Cash Margin will become part of the ANW and is one of the components that builds the embedded value.

Conclusion

6.21. We now move on to our analysis of the Cash Flow statement of the three companies, in the next chapter.

CHAPTER 7

Analysis of the Cash Flow Statement: HDFC Life, ICICI Pru, and SBI Life

Introduction

7.1. In this chapter, we will use the framework explained in the previous one and analyze the three companies. We will first tabulate the Cash Flow statement in our new format and then try to see how the companies have fared year on year. Cash Flow statements of HDFC Life, ICICI Pru and SBI Life for the years from 2012 to 2018 are used for this analysis.

Let us start our analysis with HDFC Life

Table 7.1 Ratios HDFC Life

Ratios	2018	2017	2016	2015	2014	2013	2012
comm/premium	4.67%	4.17%	4.50%	4.71%	4.32%	5.59%	5.37%
% inc in premium	21.96%	20.81%	9.72%	24.88%	5.52%	12.61%	12.42%
claims/premium	51.85%	49.89%	46.86%	53.62%	38.21%	34.08%	28.55%
% inc in operating exp	38.63%	25.40%	30.38%	1.25%	8.69%	25.29%	−31.70%
op exp/premium	13.34%	11.74%	11.31%	9.52%	11.74%	11.40%	10.24%

Source: HDFC Life annual reports

Table 7.2 Group 1 reconciliation HDFC Life

	2018	2017	2016	2015	2014	2013	2012
OPERATING CASHFLOW	67,392,824	62,302,435	56,874,645	44,593,799	54,153,778	55,264,069	56,068,530
LESS DEPRECIATION	447,087	412,417	452,241	429,799	449,311	354,951	371,443
LESS INCREASE IN PROVISIONS A	−27,349	51,085	83,371	57,860	−13,994	152,757	−13,348
PLUS PH INV INC IN REV ACCT	85,946,319	111,406,390	17,905,734	122,494,554	50,733,498	25,424,405	2,407,336
PLUS SH INV INC IN REV ACCT	2,841,224	2,303,053	1,712,131	2,033,127	1,140,773	711,532	465,915
PLUS INC IN NET CURR ASSETS D	−8,078,521	−9,180,380	−1,077,678	−839,176	2,067,254	−3,292,026	−1,618,677
LESS INC IN RES IN REV ACCT	133,222,515	160,547,546	59,281,224	156,524,996	100,583,718	68,810,173	52,445,207
LESS INC IN FUND FOR FUT APPRN	924,134	1,613,062	2,900,127	1,896,008	−1,178,200	2,185,826	−666,143
LESS PROV FOR LAPSED POLICIES	0	0	−486,811	−384,057	−2,177,983	−303,615	797,362
LESS SURP FOR DEF IN REV ACCT						601,302	1,092,625
CASH FLOW PAT	13,535,459	4,207,388	13,184,680	9,757,698	10,432,451	6,306,586	3,295,958
BALANCE SHEET PAT	11,072,030	8,869,157	8,167,868	7,855,257	7,252,819	4,514,791	2,710,154
DIFFERENCE	2,463,429	−4,661,769	5,016,812	1,902,441	3,179,632	1,791,795	585,804

Amounts in thousands.
Source: HDFC Life annual reports.

Table 7.3 *Group 1 detailed reconciliation HDFC Life*

	2018	2017	2016	2015	2014	2013	2012
PREM PLUS OTHER INCOME LESS CLAIMS LESS EXPENSES	75,125,685	68,811,563	62,481,056	48,834,058	55,472,128	56,288,298	56,872,849
INV INCOME LESS INC IN RESERVES(EXCL REINSCE)	−50,475,797	−46,189,723	−37,510,965	−33,461,140	−56,462,775	−52,775,628	−50,511,103
CASH MARGIN	24,649,888	22,621,840	24,970,091	15,372,918	−990,647	3,512,670	6,361,746
PLUS NET PAYMENT TO REINSURER	−430,751	−578,495	−434,018	−260,434	−532,853	−341,474	−355,012
PLUS REDN IN REINSURANCE RESERVES	3,800,440	499,061	−2,576,320	1,796,114	5,292,966	9,338,992	808,654
LESS INC IN FFA PAR	924,134	1,613,062	2,900,127	1,896,008	−1,178,200	2,185,826	−666,143
LESS INC IN FFA NON-PAR	0	0	−486,811	−384,057	−2,177,983	−303,615	797,362
LESS SURP FOR DEF IN REV ACCT						601,302	1,092,625
CASH BEFORE TAX	27,095,443	20,929,344	19,546,437	15,396,647	7,125,649	10,026,675	5,591,544
LESS INCOME TAX	2,477,335	2,114,395	2,166,032	1,540,435	785,497	682,755	449,307
LESS SERVICE TAX	4,928,333	3,726,459	2,773,264	1,958,794	0	0	0
PLUS ADVANCES, LOANS AND OTHER DEPOSITS	103,558	−89,779	−233,097	−480,596	0	0	0
CASH FOR SHAREHOLDERS	19,793,333	14,998,711	14,374,044	11,416,822	6,340,152	9,343,920	5,142,237
LESS DEPRECIATION	447,087	412,417	452,241	429,799	449,311	354,951	371,443
LESS INCREASE IN PROVISION A	−27,349	51,085	83,371	57,860	−13,994	152,757	−13,348
PLUS INCREASE IN NET CURRENT ASSETS D	−8,078,521	−9,180,380	−1,077,678	−839,176	2,067,254	−3,292,026	−1,618,677
PLUS INCREASE IN NET CURRENT ASSETS B	2,240,385	−1,147,441	423,926	−332,289	2,460,362	762,400	130,493
PAT FROM CASH FLOW	13,535,459	4,207,388	13,184,680	9,757,698	10,432,451	6,306,586	3,295,958
PAT FROM REVENUE ACCOUNT	11,072,030	8,869,157	8,167,868	7,855,257	7,252,819	4,514,791	2,710,154
DIFFERENCE	2,463,429	−4,661,769	5,016,812	1,902,441	3,179,632	1,791,795	585,804

Amounts in thousands.
Source: HDFC Life annual reports.

7.2. Notes

    7.2.1. There are major differences in almost all the years analyzed, except 2012, with the highest being in 2016.

    7.2.2. In 2012 and 2013, there is an additional row in the reconciliation that pertains to surplus used for deficit in the Policyholders' Revenue Account. This is peculiar to HDFC Life and is not there in the other two companies.

2012

    7.2.3. This is the first year of our analysis and is largely an uneventful year with a decent Cash for Shareholders figure.

    7.2.4. The company has reduced expenses considerably from the previous year. The claims and operating expenses (except for 2015) as a percentage of the premium are the lowest in this year when compared with all the years. This should have pushed up the Cash Margin, but this has not happened.

    7.2.5. From the Revenue Account, we can see that the investment income earned by the company is very less. This could be one of the reasons for a low Cash Margin, and the new business strain must also have made its own contribution.

    7.2.6. The company has used some part of the funds for future appropriation (FFA) par to increase profits. Since this is FFA from the par fund, 90 percent of it would have gone to the policyholders in the form of bonus.

2013

    7.2.7. The first indication of trouble is seen in this year. (Premium less claims less expenses) reduces. Cash Margin has also reduced from the previous year's figure. The ratios table indicates that this is mainly due to high claims.

    7.2.8. The reduction in reserves due to reinsurance is the highest in this year. This has the effect of pushing up profit after tax (PAT). (This is dealt with in detail later in the chapter.)

7.2.9. The company has also used a part of the lapsed policies fund to increase the Cash for Shareholders and at the same time has made a high contribution to the FFA par fund.

2014

7.2.10. This is a problem year for all the companies. (Premium less claims less expenses) has reduced a little more from the previous year. The ratios table shows that premium growth in percentage terms is at its lowest and claims as a percentage of the premium has increased slightly from the previous year.

7.2.11. Investment income earned by the company has doubled from the previous year but this has not helped to keep the Cash Margin positive, indicating that the company does not have cash even to meet its tax obligations.

7.2.12. This negative is offset by a combination of the reduction in reinsurance reserves, FFA from the par fund, and FFA from the lapsed policies fund.

7.2.13. Cash for Shareholders also registers a dip despite the above measures.

2015

7.2.14. (Premium less claims less expenses) is again lower than for the previous year. The ratios table indicates a good premium percentage increase and also a very high claims to premiums at 53 percent. The increase in premium has not managed to offset the increase in claims and increase in expenses.

7.2.15. Cash Margin, however, is a high positive number, indicating that the company has managed to make profits with the claims. The company will make an accounting profit from the claims if the reserves the company holds in respect of its claims are higher than the payment made, releasing the extra reserves into the Cash Margin. The annual report hints at high surrenders during the year, and it is obvious that the surrenders have been to the company's advantage. Companies generally make more profits from policies held to term, so this is usually not a very good sign. Whether this is good or bad is something only the company can answer. This has, however, resulted in good end year numbers.

7.2.16.   The reduction in reserves because of reinsurance is not as high as in the previous years, and the company has made a positive contribution to FFA par.

7.2.17.   Service tax is introduced this year, and it has reduced the Cash for Shareholders.

2016

7.2.18.   A very good year, with good numbers throughout (Premium less claims less expenses) has improved a lot. This is despite the fact that premium growth is not too high and there is a very high increase in expenses. This is achieved by a major reduction in the claims to premiums ratio.

7.2.19.   Cash Margin has shot up from the previous year even with a reduced investment income, and the company has made a very high contribution to FFA par.

7.2.20.   The reduction in reserves due to reinsurance are negative, indicating that the company has increased its reserves on account of reinsurance, instead of reducing them. This is unique to HDFC Life and to this particular year. This will also have the effect of bringing down the profits declared.

7.2.21.   This year the company has completely used up the FFA in the non-par fund.

2017

7.2.22.   There is an increase in the (premium less claims less expenses) figure, with a small dip in Cash Margin. The dip may be due to new business strain because the premiums have increased by 20 percent or it could be because of the increased claims ratio.

7.2.23. Reinsurance reserves are insignificant, and the company has made a fat contribution to FFA par.

7.2.24. The Cash for Shareholders is also a very healthy number.

2018

7.2.25. (Premium less claims less expenses) looks good despite the claims ratio being very poor and the expenses being very high. The increase in premiums has contributed to this.

7.2.26. Cash Margin is at its best, again indicating that either claims have been profitable to the company or the company has managed to sell products with reduced new business strain. With respect to claims, the comments are the same as for 2015.

7.2.27. Reduction in reinsurance reserves in this year is different from the previous two years and has increased significantly. As for 2013, 2014 and 2015, this will have the effect of pushing up profits. The PAT (both calculated and Revenue Account) hits its peak.

ICICI Pru

Table 7.4 Ratios ICICI Pru

Ratios	2018	2017	2016	2015	2014	2013	2012
comm/ premium	4.46%	3.00%	2.87%	3.17%	4.36%	4.51%	3.71%
% inc in premium	18.10%	18.32%	20.62%	21.72%	−8.47%	−3.04%	−20.88%
claims/ premium	57.28%	58.63%	57.77%	69.23%	82.45%	83.31%	51.18%
% inc in op expenses	3.46%	12.89%	4.84%	−4.11%	−6.79%	−1.41%	
op exp/ premium	16.49%	18.82%	19.73%	22.70%	28.82%	28.30%	27.83%

Source: ICICI Pru annual reports.

Table 7.5 Group 1 reconciliation ICICI Pru

	2018	2017	2016	2015	2014	2013	2012
OPERATING CASHFLOW	56,898,878	41,296,995	36,347,644	5,003,870	−23,692,720	−26,547,268	28,154,971
LESS DEPRECIATION	437,043	578,659	455,795	396,990	469,440	410,649	556,645
LESS INCREASE IN PROVISIONS A	16,884	27,870	30,103	12,332	36,575	−34,678	83,698
PLUS PH INV INC IN REV ACCT	112,614,697	149,769,454	12,083,680	187,244,458	92,167,437	61,804,380	−1,418,084
PLUS SH INV INC IN REV ACCT	7,419,089	6,669,783	6,018,911	5,357,684	3,897,338	4,172,973	2,207,544
PLUS INC IN NET CURR ASSETS D	−3,202,483	−6,669,975	−723,003	−247,682	1,891,869	845,991	−5,429
LESS INC IN RES IN REV ACCT	154,474,972	174,975,550	35,154,814	179,561,032	56,617,344	25,930,741	17,025,834
LESS INC IN FUND FOR FUT APPRN	2,739,745	−577,275	1,344,243	234,499	−42,153	−2,509,625	−2,129,857
CASH FLOW PAT	16,061,537	16,061,453	16,742,277	17,153,477	17,182,718	16,478,989	13,402,682
BALANCE SHEET PAT	16,191,653	16,816,612	16,501,455	16,343,916	15,655,897	14,958,350	13,841,292
DIFFERENCE	−130,116	−755,159	240,822	809,561	1,526,821	1,520,639	−438,610

Amounts in thousands.
Source: ICICI Pru annual reports.

Table 7.6 Group 1 detailed reconciliation ICICI Pru

	2018	2017	2016	2015	2014	2013	2012
PREM PLUS OTHER INCOME LESS CLAIMS LESS EXPENSES	65,905,366	49,752,770	42,226,967	8,744,434	−22,901,854	−25,800,391	28,525,138
INV INCOME LESS INC IN RESERVES(EXCL REINSCE)	−51,368,556	−47,501,511	−24,665,682	8,391,590	37,526,715	37,322,338	−19,719,973
CASH MARGIN	14,536,810	2,251,259	17,561,285	17,136,024	14,624,861	11,521,947	8,805,165
PLUS NET PAYMENT TO REINSURER	−180,822	−346,370	−308,784	−420,387	−704,627	−456,054	−429,042
PLUS REDN IN REINSURANCE RESERVES	21,232,205	23,446,270	7,063,465	2,609,515	1,470,917	1,425,291	1,988,699
LESS INC IN FFA PAR	2,739,880	1,284,188	1,212,683	513,860	1,261,956	605,098	−143,934
LESS INC IN FFA NON-PAR	−135	−1,861,463	131,560	−279,361	−1,304,109	−3,114,723	−1,985,923
CASH BEFORE TAX	32,848,448	25,928,434	22,971,723	19,090,653	15,433,304	15,000,809	12,494,679
LESS INCOME TAX	1,697,876	2,949,392	1,943,811	0	83,203	350,001	315,543
LESS SERVICE TAX	7,042,688	5,172,072	3,651,481	3,326,182	0	0	0
PLUS ADVANCES, LOANS AND OTHER DEPOSITS	−85,102	12,059	24,753	6,005	−3,036	59,178	374,418
CASH FOR SHAREHOLDERS	24,022,782	17,819,029	17,401,184	15,770,476	15,347,065	14,709,986	12,553,554
LESS DEPRECIATION	437,043	578,659	455,795	396,990	469,440	410,649	556,645
LESS INCREASE IN PROVISION A	16,884	27,870	30,103	12,332	36,575	−34,678	83,698
PLUS INCREASE IN NET CURRENT ASSETS D	−3,202,483	−6,669,975	−723,003	−247,682	1,891,869	845,991	−5,429
PLUS INCREASE IN NET CURRENT ASSETS B	−4,304,835	5,518,928	549,994	2,040,005	449,799	1,298,983	1,494,900
PAT FROM CASH FLOW	16,061,537	16,061,453	16,742,277	17,153,477	17,182,718	16,478,989	13,402,682
PAT FROM REVENUE ACCOUNT	16,191,653	16,816,612	16,501,455	16,343,916	15,655,897	14,958,350	13,841,292
DIFFERENCE	−130,116	−755,159	240,822	809,561	1,526,821	1,520,639	−438,610

Amounts in thousands.
Source: ICICI Pru annual reports.

7.3. Notes

    7.3.1. The reconciliation is a closer match than for HDFC Life, with the maximum difference in 2013.

    7.3.2. I also noticed something very peculiar to ICICI Pru that is related to the operating expenses ratio. The operating expenses and premiums are much higher in the Cash Flow statement than in the Revenue Account. The differences cancel each other out in the aforementioned Cash Flow statement reconciliation because premiums and expenses come with opposite signage. The differences between Revenue Account operating expenses and Cash Flow statement operating expenses are very similar to the Revenue Account premium and the Cash Flow statement premium after tax is netted off. Tax has to be netted off from both the Revenue Account premium and the Cash Flow statement premium because the Revenue Account premium is net of service tax only for non-linked business whereas Cash Flow statement is gross of tax. So, to compare the Revenue Account premium with the Cash Flow statement premium, tax has to be taken out from both to make the comparison reasonable. This could very well be because of some accounting policy that is different for the Cash Flow statements, but this needs to be verified with the company. This is another reason why the reconciliation for the major account heads should be done separately, that is, premiums in the Cash Flow statement must be separately reconciled with the premiums in the Revenue Account and so on. This reconciliation is almost impossible with only the information in the published accounts, but the company accounts department may be able to do this because it will have all the information.

2012

    7.3.3. There is a massive reduction in premium collected at 20 percent. This year also has a high claim to premium ratio.

ICICI Pru has the highest claims ratio in all the years among the three companies.

7.3.4. Although the investment income is negative (this is unprecedented), Cash Margin does not seem to have taken a hit when compared with that of the other companies. This suggests that claims may have pushed up the Cash Margin. The reasons are the same as discussed for HDFC Life in 2015.

7.3.5. Around 14 percent of the Revenue Account PAT is from the FFA of the non-par fund.

2013

7.3.6. The first red flag is a high negative (premium less claims less expenses). This is not seen in the other two companies in any year. Claims ratio is at 83 percent, the highest for ICICI Pru in all the years analyzed.

7.3.7. The premiums have also reduced marginally, and this means that overall, business is going off the books.

7.3.8. Cash Margin is higher than that of the previous year, and our comments remain the same as for the previous year.

7.3.9. This year the FFA contribution from the non-par fund hits an all-time high.

2014

7.3.10. This is the second year of negative (premium less claims less expenses). The premiums have reduced some more, and the claims ratio almost remains the same.

7.3.11. This year's Cash Margin has increased from the previous year's, indicating that either the claims this year are probably more profitable than those of the previous year or the new business strain has reduced or both.

7.3.12. The company has reduced the amount taken out of the FFA non-par considerably and has also made a contribution to FFA par.

2015

7.3.13. (Premium less claims less expenses) turns positive, with a reduction in the claims ratio. There is a healthy positive increase in the premiums after two years of negative premium growth.

7.3.14. The company has managed to achieve an increase in the Cash Margin, implying that the company has managed the new business strain and contributed to the profits.

7.3.15. The company has also made a positive contribution to FFA par and taken a small amount from FFA non-par.

7.3.16. The reduction because of reinsurance has inched upward from the previous year.

2016

7.3.17. The company has a good (premium less claims less expenses) figure; the claims ratio has come down some more; and the Cash Margin has registered a jump, despite the investment income not being too good.

7.3.18. The company has also increased its contribution to FFA (both par and non-par).

7.3.19. The reduction in reserves because of reinsurance is, however, more than twice as much as the previous year.

2017

7.3.20. Cash Margin has reduced considerably. This a red flag because it is out of line with the previous year and with the other companies. The ratios table says that there is a healthy increase in premiums with the claims ratio being the same as that of the previous year. This could be because of claims on unprofitable terms or the effect of new business strain. The company should have more information here, and this should be clarified with the company.

7.3.21. Reinsurance reserve reduction is at its highest and is more than thrice as much as 2016's figure. This is a major contributor to Cash before Tax.

7.3.22. The company has also taken a major amount from the FFA non-par while contributing to the FFA par.

7.3.23. The company has managed to increase its Cash before Tax and maintain the Cash for Shareholders.

2018

7.3.24. (Premium less claims less expenses) has increased, so also Cash Margin. Despite this, Cash Margin for this year is lower than the previous four years' figures. Comments for 2017 hold good for 2018 as well.

7.3.25. The reduction in reinsurance reserves has almost remained the same as for 2017, but the company has made a healthy positive contribution to FFA par and has taken only a very small sum from the FFA non-par fund.

7.3.26. Cash before Tax and PAT are the highest among the three companies.

SBI Life

Table 7.7 Ratios SBI Life

Ratios	2018	2017	2016	2015	2014	2013	2012
comm/ premium	3.99%	3.38%	4.01%	4.08%	4.63%	4.42%	3.73%
% inc in premium	19.67%	33.48%	23.36%	19.37%	3.96%	−17.76%	−2.90%
claims/ premium	45.16%	45.92%	47.39%	62.43%	80.52%	72.00%	36.77%
% inc in op expenses	17.97%	17.97%	18.99%	9.72%	−5.84%	−0.60%	13.47%
op exp/ premium	6.65%	6.74%	7.63%	7.91%	8.61%	9.50%	7.86%

Source: SBI Life annual reports.

Table 7.8 Group 1 reconciliation SBI Life

	2018	2017	2016	2015	2014	2013	2012
OPERATING CASHFLOW	103,936,668	85,251,158	57,779,358	27,148,192	1,682,697	11,299,628	64,678,743
LESS DEPRECIATION	593,054	475,586	371,245	389,200	462,841	269,002	343,191
LESS INCREASE IN PROVISIONS A	788,308	122,182	−58,471	103,980	154,193	21,695	2,982
PLUS PH INV INC IN REV ACCT	84,562,504	92,949,841	33,409,150	102,429,137	63,539,991	43,739,496	5,831,243
PLUS SH INV INC IN REV ACCT	4,520,649	4,015,594	3,177,857	2,761,137	2,021,809	1,505,195	959,963
PLUS INC IN NET CURR ASSETS D	−3,077,180	−352,142	−4,408,612	555,958	−871,507	366,877	5,828,946
LESS INC IN RES IN REV ACCT	175,949,631	172,409,642	79,868,593	122,840,767	58,807,282	47,831,860	69,177,243
LESS INC IN FUND FOR FUT APPRN	1,934,792	0	2,306	14,626	74,263	218,411	287,269
CALCULATED PAT	10,676,856	8,857,041	9,774,080	9,545,851	6,874,411	8,570,228	7,488,210
PAT	11,503,922	9,546,529	8,610,341	8,200,421	7,401,342	6,221,709	5,558,214
DIFFERENCE	−827,066	−689,488	1,163,739	1,345,430	−526,931	2,348,519	1,929,996

Amounts in thousands.
Source: SBI Life annual reports.

Table 7.9 *Group 1 detailed reconciliation SBI Life*

	2018	2017	2016	2015	2014	2013	2012
PREM PLUS OTHER INCOME LESS CLAIMS LESS EXPENSES	113,776,528	94,580,127	66,061,644	33,475,682	6,906,830	14,882,327	66,120,417
PLUS INV INCOME LESS INC IN RESERVES(EXCL REINSCE)	−91,777,990	−75,321,078	−46,707,472	−21,339,499	4,082,422	−6,866,781	−64,974,122
CASH MARGIN	21,998,538	19,259,049	19,354,172	12,136,183	10,989,252	8,015,546	1,146,295
PLUS NET PAYMENT TO REINSURER	−50,951	245,140	−672,930	−331,229	−278,326	−210,658	−119,112
PLUS REDN IN REINSURANCE RESERVES	105,135	33,769	303,647	8,520	90,051	79,990	96,125
LESS INC IN FFA PAR	1,934,792	0	0	0	0	0	0
LESS INC IN FFA NON-PAR	0	0	2,306	14,626	74,263	218,411	287,269
CASH BEFORE TAX	20,117,930	19,537,958	18,982,583	11,798,848	10,726,714	7,666,467	836,039
LESS INCOME TAX	4,818,494	4,192,808	3,452,664	2,552,390	1,874,425	540,934	196,305
LESS SERVICE TAX	5,068,524	5,051,180	3,997,625	3,443,871	3,071,384	2,831,109	1,126,259
PLUS ADVANCES, LOANS AND OTHER DEPOSITS	98,107	−330,121	−159,067	0	0	0	0
CASH FOR SHAREHOLDERS	10,329,019	9,963,849	11,373,227	5,802,587	5,780,905	4,294,424	−486,525
LESS DEPRECIATION	593,054	475,586	371,245	389,200	462,841	269,002	343,191
LESS INCREASE IN PROVISION A	788,308	122,182	−58,471	103,980	154,193	21,695	2,982
PLUS INCREASE IN NET CURRENT ASSETS D	−3,077,180	−352,142	−4,408,612	555,958	−871,507	366,877	5,828,946
PLUS INCREASE IN NET CURRENT ASSETS B	4,806,377	−156,898	3,122,239	3,680,486	2,582,045	4,199,622	2,491,960
PAT FROM CASH FLOW	10,676,854	8,857,041	9,774,080	9,545,851	6,874,409	8,570,226	7,488,208
PAT FROM REVENUE ACCOUNT	11,503,922	9,546,529	8,610,341	8,200,421	7,401,342	6,221,709	5,558,214
DIFFERENCE	−827,068	−689,488	1,163,739	1,345,430	−526,933	2,348,517	1,929,994

Amounts in thousands.
Source: SBI Life annual reports.

7.4. Notes

There is a small difference in the final row in Tables 7.8 and 7.9 due to rounding errors.

7.4.1. A reasonable match between PAT from Cash Flow and PAT from Revenue Account in three years, with the maximum difference in 2013.

7.4.2. The reduction in reserves for reinsurance is the lowest among the three companies in all the years and SBI Life's terms of reinsurance seem to be very different.

7.4.3. The FFA also is never negative (although it is negative in some of the lines of businesses), and the contribution to the profits from this source is also zero.

7.4.4. The taxation numbers are higher than ICICI Pru or HDFC Life. This is dealt with later in the chapter.

7.4.5. Operating expenses/premium: This ratio is unbelievable at around 7 percent and is at the level most companies only dream about but never achieve. The company has also managed to maintain this over the past four years. This, together with the commission ratio, proves that SBI Life has managed to keep a very tight leash on expenses, where the other two have failed miserably. This is very important because this will have a major impact on profitability. One of the reasons for the lower expenses maybe the channel of distribution. The 2018 annual report for SBI Life states that 67.4 percent of the new business is sold by bancassurance. This percentage is, with 33 percent for HDFC Life and 52.3 percent for ICICI Pru. (Please refer to Table 8.4 in chapter 8 for more details on these numbers.) Again, this cannot be viewed in isolation and is only one of the factors. Our eyes must remain constantly on the bottom line, which is the profitability to the shareholders. If by spending more, the companies are able to improve profitability, then the expenses are more than justified.

2012

7.4.6. The (premium less claims less expenses) is the highest in 2012 among the three companies, but the Cash Margin is the lowest. This could very well have been caused by new business strain as the claims ratio does not seem to be very high and expenses also seem under control. If the new business is written on profitable terms, this size of the Cash Margin should not matter.

7.4.7. Cash for Shareholders is negative, and this is not seen in any other company or in any other year for SBI Life. This should not be seen as a minus, however, if new business is written on profitable terms. The conclusions on the Cash before Tax and the Cash for Shareholders must be analyzed with these in mind.

2013

7.4.8. This is not a very good year in terms of premium collected and claims paid. The premium collected has reduced by 17 percent, and the claims ratio has shot up to 72 percent. This has brought down the premium less claims less expenses.

7.4.9. Cash Margin has, however, increased, and the comments are the same as for the other two companies.

7.4.10. SBI Life also seems to pay service tax when the other two do not.

2014

7.4.11. There is a small increase in premium collected; the claims ratio has shot up some more to 80 percent; and the (premium less claims less expenses) has come down some more. This means that the increase in premiums is not enough to match the increase in claims and expenses. Cash Margin has gone up, and the comments remain the same as for 2013.

2015

7.4.12. This is the starting year of a very high growth for the company—business has increased by leaps and bounds, and the claims ratio is well on its way down. The company has not only managed to retain its Cash Margin, but also has achieved an increase. This increase is after it has met its new business strain. It is highly likely that SBI Life does not have a new business strain at all because of its reduced operating expenses and reduced commission in the first year.

7.4.13. The net effect on the Cash for Shareholders remains almost the same as that of the previous year.

2016

7.4.14. A wonderful year in all respects. The premiums have increased by 23 percent, and there is an increase in the (premium less claims less expenses). The company has achieved a major breakthrough in the reduction in the claims ratio and has managed to keep this level in the future as well.

7.4.15. There is a huge jump in Cash Margin despite the growth in the new business, making us wonder once again about the new business strain.

7.4.16. Cash for shareholders has almost doubled.

2017

7.4.17. Premium has increased by 33 percent, probably the highest seen in any company. (Premium less claims less expenses) has also increased. This year, however, there is no major jump in the Cash Margin. This is not bad, but the previous year has upped our expectations, and it looks like the business captured is not the same as last year.

7.4.18. Cash for Shareholders has registered a small dip, as compared to the previous year.

2018

> 7.4.19. This year is very similar to 2017. Premium growth is not as high as in the previous year, but there is an increase in (premium less claims less expenses). There is also an increase in Cash Margin.
>
> 7.4.20. In this year the company has deviated from the norm and made a major contribution to FFA.
>
> 7.4.21. The Cash for Shareholders is almost the same as in the previous year.

7.5. This finishes our discussion on the Cash Flow statements, and we now move on to reinsurance and taxation.

Why is reduction in reinsurance reserves brought out separately? Should it not be grouped with the reserves and be a part of the increase in reserves?

7.6. When the company reinsures, risk is transferred from the company to the reinsurer. The life insurance companies collect premiums from the policyholder and pass on this risk to the reinsurance company by paying premiums to the reinsurance company. The premium paid to the reinsurer will be a negative in the Revenue Account, and the claims from the reinsurer will be a positive.

> 7.6.1. The effect on the Revenue Account will depend on the interaction of the reinsurance premium paid, commission collected from the reinsurance company, the claims paid by the reinsurance company, and the reserves reduced on account of reinsurance.
>
> 7.6.2. In the Cash Flow statement, the effect of reinsurance is shown as a net figure as the net paid to the reinsurer. Please note this is always a negative, except for SBI Life in 2017, which means that the premium paid to the reinsurer, net of reinsurance commission is almost always more than the claims paid by the reinsurer.

7.7. This means that there is a cost associated with reinsurance, and this can roughly be taken as the net paid to the reinsurer. This will have the effect of reducing the profits of the company reinsuring a part of its business, which in our case is the life insurance company.

7.8. Coming back to the Revenue Account, we can analyze the impact of reinsurance on the PAT by looking at only those figures in the Revenue Account that are because of reinsurance. The net increase in PAT can be written as follows:

Minus Reinsurance premium

plus Reinsurance commission

plus Reinsurance claims paid

plus Reduction in reserves because of reinsurance

= Increase in PAT

What is the reason for reducing the reserves on account of reinsurance?

7.9. Companies are allowed to hold lesser reserves if they feel that reinsurance claims will be more than the reinsurance premium they will be paying in the future. This means that the reinsurance contracts are written on very profitable terms for the company and the company expects to make money from the reinsurance arrangements. By how much the reserves can be reduced depends on the terms of the reinsurance contract, and it is the actuary's call. This has the effect of capitalizing future profits the company hopes to make.

7.10. I have calculated the percentage increase in PAT for all the three companies and expressed them in percentage terms to the PAT. This shows the extent of the increase in the PAT because of reinsurance arrangements. For the purpose of this exercise, I have considered reinsurance only in the Policyholders' Technical Account and ignored the reinsurance (if any) in the Shareholders' Non-technical Account.

Table 7.10 HDFC Life Reinsurance impact on PAT

	2018	2017	2016	2015	2014	2013	2012
REINSCE PREM	1,934,468	1,706,214	1,341,980	674,462	908,768	640,471	525,347
REINSCE COMM					44,083	78,552	
REINSCE CLAIMS	1,968,672	1,208,458	788,561	923,448	426,805	292,778	153,302
REINSCE RES	3,800,440	499,061	−2,576,320	1,796,114	5,292,966	9,338,992	808,654
INCREASE IN PAT	3,834,644	1,305	−3,129,739	2,045,100	4,855,086	9,069,851	436,609
PAT	11,072,030	8,869,157	8,167,868	7,855,257	7,252,819	4,514,791	2,710,154
% INCREASE IN PAT	35%	0%	−38%	26%	67%	201%	16%

Amounts in thousands.
Source: HDFC Life annual reports.

7.10.1. The maximum increase in PAT in percentage terms is in the year 2013 at 201 percent. This happens because of the high reduction in reserves. This means that if these reinsurance arrangements were not in place, the company would have had a deficit equal to the PAT.

7.10.2. The increase also varies by different funds in the same year. For example, in the same year (2013), the maximum reduction in reserves, and therefore, the maximum increase in the surplus is in the non-par fund. If we express the reinsurance reserves as a proportion of the premium, it is
$23,507/30,939 = 0.75$ for the individual life par fund and
$9,305,481/356,786 = 26$ for the individual and group life nonpar fund.

7.10.3. In 2016, the company has increased rather than reduced the reserves, which is unprecedented. The segmental Revenue Account states that this increase is in the non-par individual and group life and in its non-par health business. This will have the effect of bringing down the profitability of those two lines of businesses. The only year where it does not have any impact is 2017.

Table 7.11 ICICI Pru Reinsurance impact on PAT

	2018	2017	2016	2015	2014	2013	2012
REINSCE PREM	2,580,917	1,987,544	1,656,938	1,461,710	1,459,968	1,210,008	936,980
REINSCE COMM							
REINSCE CLAIMS	2,649,545	1,707,167	1,332,991	1,068,315	833,734	795,566	617,789
REINSCE RES	21,232,205	23,446,270	7,063,465	2,609,515	1,470,917	1,425,291	1,988,699
INCREASE IN PAT	21,300,833	23,165,893	6,739,518	2,216,120	844,683	1,010,849	1,669,508
PAT	16,191,653	16,816,612	16,501,455	16,343,916	15,655,897	14,958,350	13,841,292
% INCREASE IN PAT	132%	138%	41%	14%	5%	7%	12%

Amounts in thousands.
Source: ICICI Pru annual reports.

7.10.4. The years 2017 and 2018 stand out for the maximum increase in PAT. The percentage increase in 2016 is also quite high.

7.10.5. In those years, the reduction in the reserves happens only in the non-par fund, whereas reinsurance premiums are paid in both par and non-par funds. This means that the surplus in the par fund is unaffected by reinsurance and the surplus in the non-par fund carries all the benefits of lower reserves. The reinsurance premiums in the par fund are a very small percentage of the total premiums, so the changes will not be very significant.

7.10.6. This also has a direct impact on taxation because in ICICI Pru the surplus in the non-par fund does not carry a tax charge. This is dealt with in the following section on taxation.

Table 7.12 SBI Life Reinsurance impact on PAT

	2018	2017	2016	2015	2014	2013	2012
REINSCE PREM	1,941,224	1,626,819	1,599,138	871,103	814,976	679,191	528,974
REINSCE COMM							13,066
REINSCE CLAIMS	1,678,063	1,561,295	1,485,969	600,035	611,907	398,587	341,575
REINSCE RES	105,135	33,769	303,647	8,520	90,051	79,990	96,125
INCREASE IN PAT	−158,026	−31,755	190,478	−262,548	−113,018	−200,614	−78,208
PAT	11,503,922	9,546,529	8,610,341	8,200,421	7,401,342	6,221,709	5,558,214
% INCREASE IN PAT	−1%	0%	2%	−3%	−2%	−3%	−1%

Amounts in thousands.
Source: SBI Life annual reports.

7.10.7. SBI Life is the only company that has a decrease in PAT because of reinsurance in all the years save one. The reduction in reinsurance reserves is a tiny percentage of the reinsurance premium.

7.10.8. This means that SBI Life has either been very conservative in its estimates or the reinsurance arrangements are completely different for SBI Life.

7.11. It is worth noting that the reinsurance premiums in all the three companies do not vary too much.

Taxation of life insurance companies

7.12. The published information does not give us any idea about how the tax is computed, and companies only state that taxation is as per Section 44 of the Income Tax Act 1961. The details of the income tax act are beyond the scope of this book, and I have only highlighted my observations.

7.13. Tax figures in three places in the Revenue Account: the first, as a provision or charge for income tax in the Revenue Account; the second, as a service tax again in the Revenue Account; and the third, as a provision in the Shareholders' Non-technical Account. For the purpose of this analysis, I have ignored service tax and looked at only income tax.

7.14. For par business, surplus is defined as the surplus before bonus is declared.

7.15. Also, tax is levied on only some lines of businesses, so I have used the Segmental Revenue Account for this purpose and have taken only those lines of businesses that have a tax charge or a tax provision.

7.16. The companies are uniform in ignoring the pension business, which is non-taxable. As to which other funds are taxable, each of them have their own interpretation. For example, ICICI Pru has a tax charge only in the par fund, all other funds are ignored. In the Revenue Account, I have used the surplus after tax, and in the Shareholders' Non-technical Account, I have used profit before tax (PBT).

7.16.1. Let us start with HDFC Life.

Table 7.13 HDFC Life Tax in Policyholders' Technical Account

INCOME TAX	PAR LIFE	NON-PAR LIFE	NON-PAR HEALTH	UL INDL LIFE	UL GROUP	TOTAL
TAX PROVISION	1,192,252	1,007,864	45,195	−504,096	14,259	1,755,474
SURPLUS	9,591,808	5,981,483	268,220	358,902	187,018	16,387,431
TAX/ SURPLUS %	12.43%	16.85%	16.85%	−140.46%	7.62%	10.71%

Source: HDFC Life 2018 Segmental Revenue Account.

Table 7.14 HDFC Life Tax in Shareholders' Non-technical Account

TAX IN SH NON-TECH	177,412
PBT	11,249,442
TAX/PBT%	1.58%
TOTAL TAX	1,932,886

Amounts in thousands.
Source: HDFC Life 2018 Shareholders' Non-technical Account.

7.16.2. There is a negative provision in unit-linked individual life, which is more than the surplus of the group. This means that if there is no provision, there is a deficit for that line of business.

7.16.3. Total tax in the Policyholders' Technical Account is the sum of all the provisions or charges, and total surplus is the sum of the surpluses of those lines of businesses where there is a tax provision or a charge. It excludes those lines of businesses where there is no tax to be paid. This percentage of total tax in technical account/total surplus is 10.71 percent for HDFC Life.

7.16.4. Tax in the Shareholders' Non-technical Account is only 1.58 percent, much lower than that of ICICI Pru.

ICICI Pru

Table 7.15 ICICI Pru Tax in Policyholders' Technical Account

INCOME TAX	PAR LIFE
TAX CHARGE	1,200,710
SURPLUS	7,361,880
TAX/SURPLUS %	16.31%

Source: ICICI Pru 2018 Segmental Revenue Account.

Table 7.16 ICICI Pru Tax in Shareholders' Non-technical Account

TAX IN SH NON-TECH	997,367
PBT	17,188,971
TAX/PBT%	5.80%
TOTAL TAX	2,198,077

Amounts in thousands.
Source: ICICI Pru 2018 Shareholders' Non-technical Account.

7.16.5. Tax is paid only in the par life business. On other lines of businesses, no tax is paid, which is not seen in the other two companies. The tax expressed as a percentage of the surplus is also the highest in the par business among the three companies.

7.16.6. There is also a deferred tax charge in linked life fund, but it is small enough to be ignored.

7.16.7. Tax percentage in the shareholders' Non-technical Account is more than the tax percentage in the shareholders' Non-technical Account for HDFC Life and SBI Life. This percentage is 5.8 percent, the maximum among the three.

7.16.8. It is possible that ICICI Pru sums up the surplus from the policyholders' technical account and the shareholders' taxable income into one group and then allocates a tax charge to this sum. This explains the higher tax percentage in the Shareholders' Non-technical Account but does not explain why ICICI Pru pays the least amount of total tax (sum of both Revenue Account and Shareholders' Non-technical Account) despite being the market leader in premium collection and PAT.

Table 7.17 SBI Life Tax in Policyholders' Technical Account

Income Tax	PAR Life	PAR Variable	NON-PAR Life	NON-PAR GR Savings	NON-PAR GR Others	NON-PAR Annuity	Total
Tax Provision	1,452,868	187,439	285,818	103,159	341,446	9,221	2,379,951
Surplus	10,652,834	1,151,165	2,029,482	832,209	2,386,288	63,945	17,115,923
Tax/ Surplus %	13.64%	16.28%	14.08%	12.40%	14.31%	14.42%	13.90%

Source: SBI Life 2018 Segmental Revenue Account.

Table 7.18 SBI Life Tax in Shareholders' Non-technical Account

TAX IN SH NON-TECH	340,661
PBT	11,844,583
TAX/PBT %	2.88%
TOTAL TAX	2,720,612

Amounts in thousands.
Source: SBI Life 2018 Shareholders' Non-technical Account.

7.16.9. SBI Life pays the most, in terms of the actual amount of tax, despite not declaring the highest surplus (this includes surplus from all lines of business) or PAT. This may be an unfair comparison because some funds are not taxable, and it is likely that the surplus is higher in those funds for HDFC Life and ICICI Pru.

7.16.10. If we only look at taxable funds, we can only compare SBI Life with HDFC Life (because ICICI Pru has a tax charge only in the par fund and the comparison will not be like with like). Even in this case, although the two companies have declared a similar amount of surplus, the tax paid in both the Policyholders' Technical Account and the Shareholders' Non-technical Account is much higher in SBI Life. The total tax in rupee terms in SBI Life is about 40 percent more than in HDFC Life.

7.16.11. In the Shareholders' Non-technical Account, the tax when expressed as a percentage of PBT, is in between that of HDFC Life and ICICI Pru.

7.16.12. We need to get to the bottom of this, because the taxation numbers are huge and they will have a major impact on profitability.

7.17. On the face of it, reinsurance and taxation are insignificant parts of the Revenue Account and the analyst may come to the wrong conclusion that she does not gain much even if she ignores them. The food for thought is, however, if SBI Life had followed the same reinsurance arrangements and paid lesser tax, its results may have been on par or even better than those of the other two companies.

How do the companies fare against each other?

7.18. After we have looked at the companies independently, it is time to compare and contrast how the companies look when placed next to each other. For this exercise, we can pick up Cash Margin from the Cash Flow statement format. This ensures that the reinsurance arrangements and taxation are kept out of the comparison.

Table 7.19 Cash margin of HDFC Life, ICICI Pru and SBI Life

CASH MARGIN	2018	2017	2016	2015	2014	2013	2012
HDFC Life	24,649,888	22,621,840	24,970,091	15,372,918	−990,647	3,512,670	6,361,746
ICICI Pru	14,536,810	2,251,259	17,561,285	17,136,024	14,624,861	11,521,947	8,805,165
SBI Life	21,998,538	19,259,049	19,354,172	12,136,183	10,989,252	8,015,546	1,146,295

Amounts in thousands.
Source: Tables 7.3, 7.6 and 7.9.

7.19. As can be seen from the aforementioned table, it is more of a roller-coaster ride for the companies rather than a smooth progression of values from one year to the next. Cash Margin is inconclusive by itself to help form a judgment on the profitability. It merely acts as a pointer for us to dig deeper. The pointers here would be SBI Life in 2012, HDFC Life in 2013 and 2014, ICICI Pru in 2017 and 2018.

7.20. A better measure of the profitability is the value of in-force (VIF) element in the embedded value. This is the present value of the shareholders' share of the profits from the in-force business discounted to the present date. Since Cash Margin is an unrefined version of the PAT, it follows that there is a dotted line connecting Cash Margin and the VIF.

7.21. Let us first tabulate the results to aid our understanding.

Table 7.20 VIF of HDFC Life, ICICI Pru and SBI Life

VIF	2018	2017	2016
HDFC Life	103,620	82,530	69,440
ICICI Pru	117,640	94,280	84,250
SBI Life	115,970	95,414	71,259

Amounts in millions.
Source: Annual reports of HDFC Life, ICICI Pru and SBI Life.

7.21.1. HDFC Life's Cash Margin was the highest among the three, in the latest year, but its VIF is the lowest.

7.21.2. ICICI Pru's Cash Margin is very low in 2017 but its VIF does not reflect this, as it remains on par with the other companies' VIF. This may be because of the factors affecting Cash Margin discussed earlier, namely, current year's experience, profit signature of the contract, and the strength of the reserving basis.

7.21.3. The current year's experience may be one off, and the company may not have revised its assumptions for the future on the basis of this one year.

7.21.4. HDFC Life is also the only company where the difference between the calculated and the Revenue Account PAT is the highest for most of the years. The first step then is to arrive at a better reconciliation, see whether there are any changes in Cash Margin.

Conclusion

7.22. What I have tried to highlight in this chapter is that the Cash Flow statement is slightly different from the Revenue Account. By highlighting the differences, I am stressing that the Cash Flow statement is that part of the accounts that should be analyzed more than the Revenue Account.

7.23. The questions that arise from this analysis will provide more information and food for thought than a Revenue Account and Balance Sheet analysis. As I had promised earlier, this chapter would raise more questions than provide answers. The aim of this chapter is, therefore, to provide the list of questions to improve our understanding of the company and its management style.

7.24. This chapter ends my discussion of Cash Flow statements and our next port of call is the relationship between embedded value and PAT.

CHAPTER 8

Relationship between Embedded Value and Profit After Tax

Introduction

8.1. In this chapter, we look at the factors affecting the embedded value and then explore the relationship between the embedded value and profit after tax (PAT) in the Revenue Account by taking a high-level view. We also try to calculate the growth rate in the PAT that matches the embedded value. Next, we look at the change in the embedded value from one year to the next and also look at parameters that help to measure this change.

What are the Factors Affecting Embedded Value?

8.2. Let us start from the embedded value and then try and analyze the factors affecting it. The embedded values of the three companies are shown in Table 8.1.

Table 8.1 Embedded Values of HDFC Life, ICICI Pru and SBI Life

Embedded value	2018	2017	2016
HDFC Life	152,160	124,710	102,330
ICICI Pru	187,880	161,840	139,390
SBI Life	190,700	165,380	125,475

Amounts in millions.
Source: Annual reports of HDFC Life, ICICI Pru and SBI Life.

8.2.1. The size of the business written

8.2.1.1. The more premium the companies write, the higher will be the embedded value, assuming that the business they write will be profitable. Size can be measured in many ways, and here I have considered the premium from the Revenue Account (Table 8.2).

Table 8.2 Revenue Account Premiums of HDFC Life, ICICI Pru and SBI Life

Premium	2018	2017	2016
HDFC Life	233,710	192,749	161,788
ICICI Pru	268,107	221,552	189,987
SBI Life	251,601	208,525	156,655

Amounts in millions.
Source: Revenue Accounts of HDFC Life, ICICI Pru and SBI Life.

8.2.1.2. In 2018 and 2017, SBI Life has a lower premium income than ICICI Pru, but a higher embedded value. This may be because of one of the following reasons:

8.2.2. The mix of business

8.2.2.1. Some products are more profitable than others. A higher percentage of these products will increase the embedded value.

8.2.2.2. Although this is a very important aspect, there is no public information available as to which of the products are more profitable.

8.2.3. The new business margin (NBM) of the business written

8.2.3.1. This is the expected profitability of the new business written. The more the expected profitability of the business, the higher the embedded value. The NBM affects only the new business written in the year. Note that this is only the expected value of the profitability and the actual profitability will be determined when the last policy of that particular tranche of business goes off the books.

8.2.3.2. If a company writes lesser volumes but with very high NBM, it may have a higher embedded value. The NBM is usually quoted for a company as a whole, but within one company it should vary a lot by distribution channel, product, and so on, and therefore, can be split into different categories. Again, this information is not publicly available (Table 8.3).

Table 8.3 NBM's of HDFC Life, ICICI Pru and SBI Life

NBM	2018	2017	2016
HDFC Life	23.2%	21.6%	19.9%
ICICI Pru	16.5%	10.1%	8.0%
SBI Life	16.2%	15.4%	14.2%

Source: Annual reports of HDFC Life, ICICI Pru and SBI Life.

8.2.3.3. The NBM has increased for all the companies, ICICI Pru more drastically than both HDFC Life and SBI Life. ICICI Pru NBM has increased by 60 percent from 2017 to 2018. It would be interesting to know what the company has done in one year to increase its expected profitability by 60 percent. In 2018, though, this NBM is more in line with its immediate competitor, SBI Life and has narrowed the gap considerably with HDFC Life. Probably, ICICI Pru has brought out new products, changed its distribution channel, and so on.

8.2.4. The distribution channel

8.2.4.1. An ideal company is one that procures good quality business without spending too much. For example, *bancassurance* is generally considered a cheaper way to sell compared with other channels. An increased business from this channel may bring down new business strain and also increase profitability.

8.2.4.2. All three companies have banks associated with their brand name and have stated in their latest annual reports (2018) that they are working on increasing business sold through bancassurance. Table 8.4 shows their progress over three years.

Table 8.4 Percentage of business sold through bancassurance

Bancassurance	2018	2017	2016
HDFC Life	33.0%	32.0%	40.0%
ICICI Pru	52.3%	56.9%	57.3%
SBI Life	67.4%	64.7%	60.7%

8.2.4.3. HDFC Life and ICICI Pru data is for the total new business premium collected and SBI Life data relates to only the individual new business premium collected. Almost 50 percent of HDFC Life's new business premium relates to group business, whereas the corresponding percentage in ICICI Pru is less than 3 percent for all the three years. To compare like with like, we have to split the above a data some more, into comparable subgroups, but this information is not publicly available.

8.2.5. Expenses of the company

8.2.5.1. Generally, the lower the expenses, the higher the embedded value. This may not always hold good, because the company may be able to increase profitability with higher expenses. This is related to the point where I have discussed the distribution channel, as the distribution channel has a direct impact on expenses.

8.2.5.2. We can compare the operational expenses as a percentage of the premium for all the three companies (Table 8.5). These figures are from Tables 7.1, 7.4 and 7.7 in Chapter 7.

Table 8.5 Operating expenses as a percentage of premium in Cash Flow statement

Operating expenses %	2018	2017	2016
HDFC Life	13.3%	11.7%	11.3%
ICICI Pru	16.5%	18.8%	19.7%
SBI Life	6.6%	6.7%	7.6%

Source: Tables 7.1, 7.4 and 7.7.

8.2.5.3. SBI Life has the least expenses as a percentage of premium. This could very well be because of a high percentage of business sold through bancassurance and also could be one of the factors for their higher embedded value.

8.2.6. Persistency, mortality, and claims experience

8.2.6.1. Generally speaking, the longer the policy remains in the books, more will be the profit made by the company, although there may be exceptions to this. This experience may be analyzed in multiple ways and companies have ongoing experience studies to address any issues that need to be corrected.

8.2.6.2. This point is also related to the profit signature of the contracts already in the company's books. These are not made public, so there is very little an analyst can do other than look at past claims experience and read the annual reports.

8.2.7. Strength of the reserves

8.2.7.1. The stronger the reserves, the later the profit emerges (which gets discounted more to the present date), and therefore, the lower is the embedded value.

A High-Level View of the Embedded Value

8.3. In simple terms, the embedded value is the present value of the shareholders' share of future profits, for business currently in the books. The dividends the shareholders receive, therefore, have a direct relationship with the embedded value of the company because only a company that declares profits will be able to pay dividends to its shareholders. In this section, I have tried to generalize the relationship between PAT and the embedded value of the company.

8.4.   In Chapter 3 on embedded value, I have explained that

$$IEV = ANW + VIF$$

Where IEV is the Indian embedded value
ANW is the adjusted net worth and
VIF is the value of in-force policies.

Since the future profits will come in only from the in-force policies, I have considered only the VIF in this section.

Coming to the PAT, it is the sum of the profits from the Policyholders' Technical Account and the profits from the Shareholders' Non-technical Account. The Policyholders' Technical Account sums up the company's current year's experience for the in force policies and transfers the shareholders' share of surplus into the Shareholders' Non-technical Account. This transferred shareholders' share of surplus therefore bears a direct relationship to the value of in force policies.

Value of In Force (VIF)

8.5.   VIF can also be expressed as

TTS in year $1 \times (1 - DDT) \times$ discount factor for year $1 + TTS$ in year $2 \times (1 - DDT) \times$ discount factor in year $2 + \ldots$ and so on until the last policy runs off the books.

Where TTS is the transfers made from the Policyholders' Technical Account to the Shareholders' Non-technical Account, DDT is the dividend distribution tax, assumed to remain the same year after year (since this surplus will ultimately be subject to DDT at the time of dividend payment), and discount factor is the present value for each of the years, assuming a constant rate of interest.

8.6. I have modified the above equation to

> VIF = estimated TTS of the year1 × (1 − DDT) × discount factor for 1 year 1+ estimated TTS of year 2 × (1 − DDT)× discount factor for 2 years + estimated TTS of the year 3 × (1 − DDT) × discount factor for 3 years and so on.

8.7. At this point I make two assumptions: The TTS grows every year from the current year at rate g and the average policy is for 20 years. The above equation then becomes

> VIF = TTS × (1 + g) × (1 − DDT) × disc factor for 1 year + TTS (1 + g) ^ 2 × (1 − DDT) × discount factor for 2 years + ... + TTS × (1 + g) ^ 20 × (1 − DDT) × discount factor for 20 years,

where TTS is the figure from the latest Shareholders' Non-technical Account and g is the rate of growth of that PAT.

> VIF = (TTS × (1 − DDT)) × ((1 + g)/(1 + i) + ((1 + g)/(1 + i)) ^ 2 + ...+ ((1 + g)/(1 + i)) ^ 20)
>
> VIF/(TTS × (1 − DDT)) = discount factor 1 + discount factor 2 + ... + discount factor 20

at a new rate of interest which is (i − g)/(1 + g), where i is the interest rate assumption for the future and g is the growth rate. In this equation, both i and g are unknown.

8.8. Here, g is the rate at which the TTS has to grow each year for the company to achieve the embedded value. The factor (i − g)/(1 + g) is more important than i or g separately. This is the factor on which my conclusions are based. The trend in this factor from one year to the next for one company and the relative difference between factors in a single year for all the companies are more important than the absolute value of the factor.

How do we use the factor $(i - g)/(1 + g)$?

8.9. For all the three companies, we have the VIF figures, which immediately show which company has the most profitable in-force business. What they do not show, however, is the relationship VIF has with the TTS of the corresponding year. This is where the $(i - g)/(1+g)$ comes in, and it shows us how this TTS is expected to move year on year to match the VIF, if TTS is projected for 20 years. This will give us a ballpark growth rate in TTS of what the companies expect, because both the VIF and the TTS are from the company's accounts. The biggest advantage of $(i - g)/(1 + g)$ is that it raises red flags and prompts us to probe further.

8.10. $(i - g)/(1 + g)$ is a very simplistic way of looking at the growth in TTS. In practice, the future TTS, and therefore, the VIF are affected by many factors listed in the previous section, and it is too simplistic to assume that all of this can be explained by only one factor, g.

8.11. The factor $(i - g)/(1 + g)$ has some limitations, for example, the following.

    8.11.1. New business affects the numerator and the denominator in different ways. When a company writes new business, VIF increases, but TTS decreases. This will distort the ratio if the percentage of new business is different in this year as opposed to the previous one. The ratio will also get distorted if the mix of new business changes, because different products will have different new business strains.

    8.11.2. The comparison leaves no room for subjectivity. For example, one company may opt to be more conservative in its embedded value assumptions and may not project very high profits. Another may choose to be aggressive. In this case, all other factors remaining the same, the conservative company's $(i - g)/(1 + g)$ would be much higher than the aggressive company's $(i - g)/(1 + g)$.

    8.11.3. TTS is affected by transfers to and from FFA and this affects the timing of surplus distribution. This also means that TTS for the year is an adjusted figure, but it has to be left unchanged to reflect actual constraints on surplus distribution.

8.11.4.   TTS is also affected by how the company calculates tax. As explained in chapter 7, tax calculation is not uniform across companies. The calculation of surplus will therefore be different depending on the methodology.

8.12.   In spite of the drawbacks of the factor mentioned above, the factor does give us a high-level view of the business. It links the revenue account to the embedded value, and therefore, attempts to connect the accounting and the actuarial aspects of the business. For now, we will only consider the direction in which this moves from one year to the next and how it varies from one company to another.

8.13.   Let us look at $(i - g)/(1 + g)$ for the last three years for all the three companies (Tables 8.6–8.8).

Table 8.6 HDFC Life factor $(i - g)/(1 + g)$

	2018	2017	2016
VIF	103,620	82,530	69,440
TTS × (1 − DDT)	7,988	6,267	5,724
(i − g)/(1 + g)	4.53%	4.36%	5.32%

Amounts in millions Source: VIF and TTS are from HDFC Life's annual reports. DDT is assumed to be 20.3 percent. (i − g)/(1 + g) is calculated.

Table 8.7 ICICI Pru

	2018	2017	2016
VIF	117,640	94,280	84,250
TTS × (1 − DDT)	8,681	9,018	9,625
(i − g)/(1 + g)	4.03%	7.17%	9.60%

Amounts in millions Source: VIF and TTS are from ICICI Pru's annual reports. DDT is assumed to be 20.3 percent. (i − g)/(1 + g) is calculated.

Table 8.8 SBI Life

	2018	2017	2016
VIF	115,970	95,414	71,259
TTS × (1 − DDT)	6,610	5,217	5,305
(i − g)/(1 + g)	1.28%	0.87%	4.13%

Amounts in millions. Source: 2016 and 2017 figures are from SBI Life's red herring prospectus. Rest are from SBI Life's annual reports. DDT is assumed to be 20.3 percent. (i - g)/(1 + g) is calculated.

8.13.1. For all the three companies, let us assume (so that the explanation becomes easier) that i is 15 percent for all the three years. In practice, i, g, TTS, and VIF are all variable. The growth g then becomes as in Table 8.9.

Table 8.9 *Calculated growth rate "g" for a fixed "i" of 15 percent*

	2018	2017	2016
HDFC Life	10.01%	10.20%	9.19%
ICICI Pru	10.54%	7.31%	4.93%
SBI Life	13.54%	14.01%	10.44%

8.13.2. Let us start with 2018. Both ICICI Pru and SBI Life have almost the same VIF, with HDFC Life not too far behind. The premiums written are very similar too. The VIF, therefore, states that the profits expected from the business written till date in all the three companies (especially for ICICI Pru and SBI Life) are the same. The TTS, however, are very different. This difference in TTS is brought out by $(i - g)/(1 + g)$. This indicates that some of the following are true.

a. TTS of the current year in ICICI Pru and HDFC Life are too high or TTS of SBI Life is too low in 2018.

b. ICICI Pru and HDFC Life may have conservative assumptions in the projections and/or SBI Life may have very optimistic assumptions.

c. In all the three years, VIF of SBI Life is higher than that of HDFC Life, but the corresponding TTS are lower. The expected future TTS of SBI Life has to be higher than expected future TTS of HDFC Life if the VIF calculations reflect the true profitability.

d. There is a huge increase in "g" in SBI Life for 2017 from 2016. This is because, in 2017, premium income has increased by 33 per cent, increasing the VIF with almost no impact on TTS. On the other hand, if we look at ICICI Pru from 2016 to 2018, the TTS has reduced from 2016 to 2018, but the VIFs are increasing year on year. This again is brought out by an increase in "g" year on year.

If the TTS are not out of line, then any of the factors discussed in the embedded value section may be the reason for the difference. These may be new business strain, profit signatures, mortality or lapse experience, strength of the reserves, and so on. This difference is brought out by $(i - g)/(1 + g)$, and it is up to the analyst to find out the reasons for this.

Change in the Embedded Value From One Year to the Next

8.14. One year down the line, the embedded value will change. This will have to be shown in the annual report, and I have put in the HDFC Life 2018 change in embedded value (see page 118) to explain this further.

8.15. The reasons for the change:

8.15.1. The company would have earned interest on the embedded value at the beginning of the year. This is the interest component and is also known as unwinding of the discount rate. Only the interest the company expected to earn is accounted for here. The actual interest earned over the year would be different and this difference between the actual and expected will form part of the economic variances in the following point 8.15.5.

8.15.2. The company may have changed its operating assumptions for the future. Operating assumptions mean mortality, expenses, morbidity, and so on. It may have fresh estimates for future years. This would be zero if assumptions remain unchanged. In addition to the operating assumptions, the company will also have economic assumptions such as interest rate, inflation. The changes from these variables are analyzed in point 8.15.5 and grouped with the investment experience of the company that is not accounted for in 8.15.1.

- **Analysis of change in EV[1]**

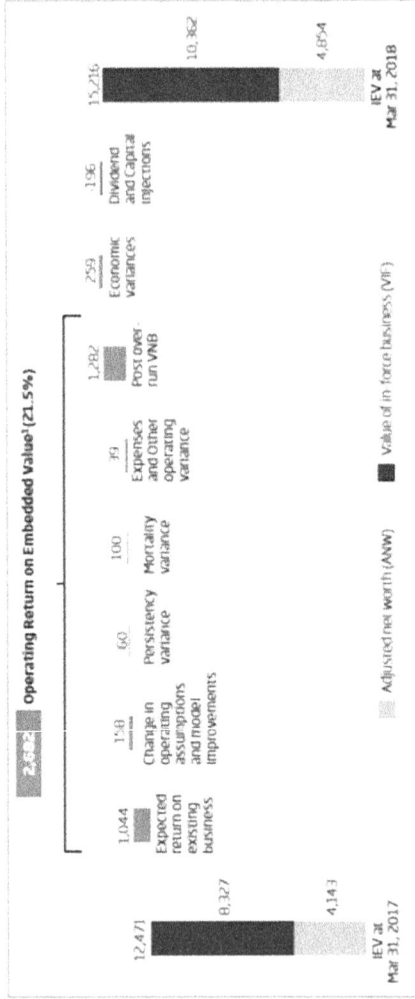

Operating Return on Embedded Value[1] (21.5%)

IEV at Mar 31, 2017	12,471
Expected return on existing business	1,044
Change in operating assumptions and model improvements	158
Persistency variance	60
Mortality variance	100
Expenses and other operating variance	19
Post over-run VNB	1,282
Economic variances	259
Dividend and Capital injections	196
IEV at Mar 31, 2018	15,216

8,327 — 4,143 (Mar 31, 2017)
10,362 — 4,854 (Mar 31, 2018)

Legend: Adjusted net worth (ANW) | Value of in force business (VIF)

Note:
1 Calculated as EVOP (Embedded Value Operating Profit) to Opening EV

8.15.3. The company would have written new business. This will straightaway increase the embedded value.

8.15.4. The current year's experience, such as mortality, expenses, morbidity, is known and the effect of the difference between the actual and the expected is put here.

8.15.5. Economic assumptions and investment variance are reported separately. Interest rate and inflation assumptions form part of the economic assumptions. The change in the embedded value arising due to changes in these assumptions is reported here. This part would also include the difference between the expected investment income and the actual investment income earned over the year. The split between the change in the embedded value because of a change in the future economic assumptions and the change in the embedded value because of the current year's investment experience is not available. Only if the future economic assumptions at the end of the year are the same as those at the beginning of the year, this part of the embedded value change along with 8.5.1 will be the total investment income earned over the year.

8.15.6. The company may have paid dividends and/or brought in capital over the year. The dividends will reduce the embedded value and the capital will increase it.

How is this Change Measured in the Company Accounts?

8.16. The company uses the embedded value of operating profits (EVOP) to measure this change. This is defined as a measure of the increase in the EV during any given period, excluding the impact on EV due to external factors like changes in economic variables and shareholder-related actions like capital injection or dividend payouts. This is then the sum of points 8.15.1 to 8.15.4 above.

8.17. Operating return on embedded value (OREV) is EVOP/EV at the beginning of the year.

8.18. The performance of the company management is sometimes measured using the OREV. The reason for excluding the economic variances is that economic variables, like interest rates, are often outside the control of the company's management and to judge them on the basis of this fluctuating measure is not seen as fair. What this measure does is that it presents a picture that does not fluctuate too much from one year to the next because of the financial environment.

8.19. It would be an interesting exercise for us, however, to find out how the company has fared using the actual interest rate earned over the year instead of the expected interest rate. This would mean that we have to add 8.15.5 to the EVOP. We have to bear in mind that we are either over estimating or under estimating the total investment income earned over the year depending on how the future economic assumptions affect the embedded value. Ideally, we should exclude the economic variances and add only the investment income of the current year. This information, however, is not available. It would also be interesting to see what is the effect of excluding the economic factors altogether. For this, we have to exclude 8.15.1 from EVOP. . I now define OREV1 and OREV2, where

8.19.1. OREV1 is the EVOP plus the change due to economic variances, expressed as a percentage of the embedded value at the beginning of the year.

OREV1 = (EVOP + economic variances)/EV at the beginning of the year

8.19.2. OREV2 is a measure of how successful the management has been in procuring new business and managing the existing business

OREV2 = (EVOP – expected return on existing business) /EV at the beginning of the year

8.20. I have calculated both OREV1 and OREV2 for all the three companies (Table 8.10).

Table 8.10 OREV, OREV1 and OREV2

	EVOP	EV beg	OREV	ECON VAR	EVOP1	OREV1	EXP RETURN	EVOP2	OREV2
HDFC Life 2018	26,820	124,710	21.51%	2,590	29,410	23.58%	10,440	16,380	13.13%
HDFC Life 2017	21,440	102,330	20.95%	2,480	23,920	23.38%	9,440	12,000	11.73%
ICICI Pru 2018	36,800	161,840	22.74%	1,130	37,930	23.44%	13,720	23,080	14.26%
ICICI Pru 2017	22,950	139,390	16.46%	5,820	28,770	20.64%	12,210	10,740	7.71%
SBI Life 2018	29,550	165,380	17.87%	–1,810	27,740	16.77%	14,060	15,490	9.37%
SBI Life 2017	28,870	125,475	23.01%	12,830	41,700	33.23%	10,860	18,010	14.35%

All amounts in millions.
Source: Annual reports of HDFC Life, ICICI Pru and SBI Life.

8.21.   ICICI Pru and HDFC Life would be more than willing to include the changes in the economic variances in the OREV because it is a positive figure for both the companies in both the years. This may not be the case in each and every year.

8.22.   For SBI Life, however, the story is a bit different.

    8.22.1.   OREV1 changes from 33.23 percent in 2017 to 16.77 percent in 2018, a change the management would find it almost impossible to explain to the shareholders. This is because in the first year the economic variances have contributed a high positive figure of 12,830, and in the next year, the contribution is a negative 1,810.

    8.22.2.   Only SBI Life has a negative economic assumptions and investment variance figure, and the company will find it difficult to explain this when both HDFC Life and ICICI Pru have positive economic variance figures.

    8.22.3.   The OREV2 figure also has reduced for SBI Life, but increased for HDFC Life and ICICI Pru.

    8.22.4.   One can only guess the mayhem that would follow in the stock market the very next day if these results are made public. On the other hand, if only the OREV figure is quoted in the accounts, the blow is softened to a very large extent, as it falls from 23 percent to 17.86 percent. This year's OREV figure is, however, not mentioned in the accounts.

Conclusion

8.23.   In this book, I have looked at only some parts of the companies' annual reports and tried to make some financial sense. The annual reports and accounts constitute a treasure trove of information and contain so much more information than what I have used here, and it would not be wrong to state that the analysis in this book is just the tip of the iceberg.

About the Author

Prasanna Rajesh is a fellow of the Institute and Faculty of Actuaries (FIA), U.K. She has more than 10 years' experience in the Indian life insurance industry. She was one of the team members involved in forecasting the capital requirements for a newly formed life insurance company in India. She is now on a long break from work and has used this opportunity to analyze the published accounts of life insurance companies from an outsider's point of view.

Index

OTHER TITLES IN OUR FINANCE AND FINANCIAL MANAGEMENT COLLECTION

John A. Doukas, Old Dominion University, *Editor*

- *Global Mergers and Acquisitions, Second Edition: Combining Companies Across Borders, Volume I* by Abdol S. Soofi and Yuqin Zhang
- *Global Mergers and Acquisitions, Second Edition: Combining Companies Across Borders, Volume II* by Abdol S. Soofi
- *Risk and Win!: A Simple Guide to Managing Risks in Small and Medium-Sized Organizations* by John Harvey Murray
- *Essentials of Financial Risk Management: Practical Concepts for the General Manager* by Rick Nason and Brendan Chard
- *Essentials of Enterprise Risk Management: Practical Concepts of ERM for General Managers* by Rick Nason and Leslie Ieming
- *Frontiers of Risk Management, Volume I: Key Issues and Solutions* by Dennis Cox
- *Frontiers of Risk Management, Volume II: Key Issues and Solutions* by Dennis Cox
- *The Art and Science of Financial Modeling* by Anurag Singal
- *Escape from the Central Bank Trap, Second Edition: How to Escape From the $20 Trillion Monetary Expansion Unharmed* by Daniel Lacalle
- *Mastering Options: Effective and Profitable Strategies for Traders* by Philip Cooper
- *Understanding Cryptocurrencies: The Money of the Future* by Arvind Matharu
- *Trade Credit and Financing Instruments* by Lucia Gibilaro
- *Trade Credit and Risk Management* by Lucia Gibilaro
- *Understanding Momentum in Investment Technical Analysis* by Micheal C. Thomsett

Announcing the Business Expert Press Digital Library

Concise e-books business students need for classroom and research

This book can also be purchased in an e-book collection by your library as

- a one-time purchase,
- that is owned forever,
- allows for simultaneous readers,
- has no restrictions on printing, and
- can be downloaded as PDFs from within the library community.

Our digital library collections are a great solution to beat the rising cost of textbooks. E-books can be loaded into their course management systems or onto students' e-book readers. The **Business Expert Press** digital libraries are very affordable, with no obligation to buy in future years. For more information, please visit **www.businessexpertpress.com/librarians.** To set up a trial in the United States, please email **sales@businessexpertpress.com.**

www.ingramcontent.com/pod-product-compliance
Lightning Source LLC
Chambersburg PA
CBHW061330220326
41599CB00026B/5111